The Effective
Student Activities Program

The Effective
STUDENT
ACTIVITIES
PROGRAM

Muriel S. Karlin

Regina Berger

Parker Publishing Company, Inc. West Nyack, N. Y.

PRINTED IN THE UNITED STATES OF AMERICA
ISBN—0-13-246454-3
B&P

Dedication

To the parents, and to our colleagues shouldering responsibilities that become evermore grave and complex, and to the children of every race, creed, color or standing—and particularly to those whose lives are blighted by poverty—we dedicate this book with deep affection, empathy and understanding.

Other Books by the Authors

EXPERIENTIAL LEARNING: AN EFFECTIVE TEACHING PROGRAM
FOR THE ELEMENTARY SCHOOLS
Parker Publishing Company, West Nyack, N.Y.

SUCCESSFUL METHODS FOR TEACHING THE SLOW LEARNER
Parker Publishing Company, West Nyack, N.Y.

SURVIVAL INSTRUCTIONS FOR THE TEACHER
Cawther Press, N.Y., N.Y.

The Purpose of This Book

An effective student activities program enables us to add extra dimensions to the education of children. Through this program we are able to meet the demands for many services which we have not yet offered, and we are able to expand the horizons of both our youngsters and our teachers. At a time when many young people are clamoring for a voice in the operation of their schools, we can offer it to them—even before we are asked. Through an active, democratically conducted student organization (usually known as the "G.O." or General Organization), supplemented by class elections and representation, we have our children participating in the planning of their educational programs—having their "say"—from the very start.

The student activities program is a force which will build feelings of camaraderie between children and teachers. This, too, is most timely and absolutely essential. We can throw open the doors of creativity through an extensive variety of clubs, meeting after school or during the day. The talents and interests of our young are developed, and they are taught to use their leisure time gainfully and pleasurably. Through various teams, physical as well as intellectual proclivities are recognized, encouraged and strengthened. Many children whose talents are athletic rather than intellectual will find recognition in this manner, and will emerge with feelings of greater self-worth. Furthermore, a boy on the basketball team does not drop out of school. Indeed, he may achieve the popularity and self-confidence that is so soul-satisfying for everyone. Cooperation too, is fostered—between students, and also between student and faculty. Just as boys enjoy participation on teams, girls love to be cheerleaders or boosters. The morale and school spirit engendered by these activities cannot be overestimated. As a result, school becomes a place of enjoyment—for many children who might otherwise be disruptive.

Because there are children with learning problems in every school, an after-school tutorial program is recommended so that these children get the additional assistance they so desperately need. By having student tutors, we supply aid, and we also train some of our young people—giving them a realistic sample of our profession. Many boys and girls may "find themselves" in this way. A give and take between students and their teachers, on a one-to-one basis, makes for greater understanding and for friendship, and for a realization that knowledge is a common reservoir from which all may draw. Adult tutoring, too, is important, to bring together teacher and student. Parents and other members of the community may be invited to participate in this program as well.

To broaden the horizons of the young, trips are suggested as part of the student activities program. These, too, have real value, in terms of increasing the children's interest in school, and in terms of developing rapport with their teachers. School magazines and newspapers fulfill the needs of the academically oriented children, whose self-worth is increased as they see their work in print.

What about the quiet child—the one with the few friends? In the production of a school play, or a concert, a trip or a festival, many friendships are made as children work or play together. In operating an effective evening school program, the parents and other members of the community may be invited to share in the student activities program—either as teachers of courses, or as students *in* them. Courses taken by adults and children, together, help to foster friendships between them. Parents and other adults can do a great deal more to develop a good student activities program by taking an active part in improving conditions in the school, by running clubs, and by helping to supply the funds for the "extras."

Our schools often lie fallow for many hours a day. Why not use them full-time? There are boys and girls who desperately need places to go and things to do. Why not open our doors to them?

You will find in this book a huge variety of student activities, with techniques for setting them up and for operating them. Every child, you will find, will, in some way, benefit from this program. Moreover, and most important, we believe a full, varied student activities program is a most desirable antidote for the anti-social feelings that form the basis for controversy in so many schools.

MURIEL S. KARLIN

REGINA BERGER

ACKNOWLEDGMENTS

Among the many persons to whom we are indebted for their cooperation in the preparation of this manuscript, we wish to thank particularly the following:

Mr. Maurice Wollin, Community Superintendent, District 31, Staten Island, New York.

Mrs. Helen Harris, Educational and Vocational Counselor, Public School 82, Manhattan.

Mr. Norman H. Harris, Principal, Anning S. Prall Junior High School, Staten Island, New York.

Many photographs were supplied by the Office of Education Information Services and Public Relations, Board of Education, City of New York. Superintendent Jerome Kovalcik has been most helpful, and we wish to publicly thank photographers John Kane and John Fulner.

Our manuscript was typed most conscientiously by Mrs. Mary Davies, of Public School 39, Statent Island. The long and arduous task of proof-reading was done by Dr. Leonard Karlin, and by Mr. Henry Karlin. Some drawings and photographs are the work of Miss Lisa Karlin. Many of our colleagues, whose names are not mentioned here, have furnished excellent ideas that have enriched this book; to them, too, we extend our appreciation.

And above all, we are indebted to the children we are privileged to work with, and who are, really, the reason-for-being of this book.

Table of Contents

4 ***Determining Which Clubs Your Students Want—and Making Them Succeed*** . . . .*(Cont.)*

5 ***Athletic Teams and Cheerleaders*** 101

6 ***The Tutorial Program*** 112

The Effective
Student Activities Program

Planning an Effective 1
Student Activities Program

An effective student activities program will pay huge dividends to students, teachers, parents and administrators—benefits far greater than the investment incurred. What then is an effective program? It consists of all of the extracurricular activities in which the student and faculty of a school are engaged. These include school and class governments, a vital club program, athletic teams, a tutorial program, student publications, entertainments such as plays and concerts, and an after-school center.

An interested, involved student government, various teams and cheerleaders, clubs and a recreation center will increase school spirit and raise the morale of everyone concerned. The children's lives will be enriched by a diversity of clubs, by trips and by class organizations, for they are given the opportunity and encouraged to be eager participants rather than spectators. For those boys and girls who need academic help, a tutorial program, both during and after school, makes it easily possible to obtain such assistance. Subscribing to the theory that the individuals who must obey rules must also be instrumental in making them, we feel young people must have a "say" in the manner in which their school is run. This is done most effectively by representative student government, both on a schoolwide and classwide scale.

For these reasons, plus many others, we believe you will find any and all ventures you make in the direction of an improved student activities program worthy of your support and commitment.

DETERMINING THE CHILDREN'S NEEDS— AND HOW THIS PROGRAM CAN HELP TO FULFILL THEM

Children need a supervised place for recreation. Some of them have a great deal of energy—and they need legitimate outlets for it. When playgrounds are unavailable, or not usable because of cold weather, an after-school center fulfills this need.

Boys and girls need to make friends and to socialize—but with adult supervision. Clubs, after-school recreation centers, even libraries and study halls accomplish this.

The "latch-key" child, whose parents work and who goes home to an empty house, needs a place between the hours of 3:00 and 5:00 (or 6:00) p.m. where he is welcome and where there are others to talk to who are interested in him. His physical safety is a factor which concerns us all. Centers must provide reliable and competent adult supervision, for it is these children who are so often the youngsters who become involved in anti-social behavior with other boys and girls in similar circumstances. Because of the lack of parental or familial supervision, they get into difficulties. They may smoke, drink beer or stronger alcoholic drinks, or even become drug users. Very often the empty apartment is an inducement to undesirable experimentation.

If we can offer this child a place where he feels comfortable and welcome, where he may play pool or ball, or just talk, are we not serving him well? Are we not administering to a deep human need?

Many children need acceptable places to meet other boys and girls. The contacts one makes in school are most important—and yet a great many of our boys and girls are acquainted with only their classmates.

There are many youngsters, living in upper economic suburbs, who have no friends in the immediate area. The "poor little rich boy" or "girl" may have to wait until he goes to college to make friends. We can be instrumental in enriching his life by extending his contacts with other children—in school.

A Quiet Place

"Hey, maw, make Johnny keep quiet."

"I have a right to sing if I want to."

"But, I'm trying to do my homework."

"So—you're supposed to concentrate."

Concentration can be extremely difficult with five children in one room—or with two in one room, if the television set is turned on, or the phonograph is blaring.

For children living in these circumstances, is it not advisable for us to provide the quiet place they need? Perhaps it is the library, or a classroom, but wherever it is—doesn't this child, too, deserve a "break"?

THE PSYCHOLOGICAL NEEDS OF CHILDREN

Young people need desperately to feel they are members of a group. Most often the "loner" is an unhappy person, craving companionship and recognition. The school supplies one group (the class) immediately, but very often he is isolated from the children in his class for one reason or another. If there are other groups he can join, such as clubs or after-school centers, he has opportunities to find companionship with other children with whom he may, perhaps, have more in common. The relaxed spirit, too, found in these centers is conducive to the making of friendships.

Peer Acceptance

By observing the dress of many of our young people, one can readily see the manifestation of the deep need for recognition by one's peers. (What could be more conforming today than the "nonconformists"?) In working together in clubs, on various teams, on publications, and in playing together, this need for acceptance is fulfilled.

Many children who have never been made to feel important before, especially in areas of academic achievement, may, overnight, be given huge morale boosts by fine performances on the baseball team. This may change their personalities completely for the better, possibly throughout their lives.

Belonging to a team, almost in itself, is peer acceptance, since the good of the team is paramount, and each player bears this in mind.

Members of the team learn social rather than anti-social behavior—that cooperation is the essence of teamwork, and that the individual must subordinate his own impulses to the needs and welfare of the team. What better lesson in democracy can we teach? Furthermore, this is learned willingly, and accepted imperceptibly—"All for one, and one for all."

For the many children who thirst for love and affection, this need can be partially fulfilled by the leader of a club or team. If a child has no parents, or lacks one, or if he does not relate well to his parents, he may be seeking a father or mother figure away from home. Furthermore, this person is not thrust upon him—he is sought out by the child himself. His attendance at these club centers is not mandatory. He comes voluntarily, and for this reason it is much more likely to have a salutary effect on him.

Every human being must, in order to have a healthy self-image, achieve success in some area. Clubs, and teams, publications and performances, give ample opportunity for the child to do something which awakens admiration. What could be more heartening for the growing child than to see his work or his feats or his skills admired?

Here, too, the child who rarely succeeds is given a chance to find himself. Anti-social behavior is discouraged and talents and skills are awakened.

It is much more likely that success will be achieved by a boy or girl in an activity which he himself has chosen, rather than in one which has been thrust upon him. His attendance will not be reluctant, and his energies will flow freely.

Security

If a child does not feel secure at home, if there is a lack of harmony, if parents or other members of the family are physically or mentally ill, the clubs or after-school centers offer a haven to him. First of all, he can feel safe, emotionally as well as physically. The deft leader gears the children toward a harmonious relationship which the insecure child craves. It is even possible, depending upon the craft of the leader, to give the child some feeling of security—a feeling that his home has been unable to furnish.

Obtaining Skills and Knowledge

Obviously a tutorial program supplements the regular school curriculum, benefiting both the giver and the taker. Children who need skills are given additional opportunities to learn them, in a relaxed and friendly environment, easly achieved in a center. There are no examinations, no competition, no harsh words spoken, no shortcomings cited, and a spirit of warmth and camaraderie is easily achieved. This informal teaching situation could succeed academically where the atmosphere in the classroom might fail. Mental blocks are not as likely to form, and ideas will flow more freely.

BRINGING OUT ENTHUSIASM OF CHILDREN

A well-developed student activities program gives the children many goals. They may be immediate or relatively remote, but for the program to be successful, there must be actual goals which can be achieved. For example, the student government can write its own constitution, carry on campaigns and elect its officers, and actually meet with the administrators to discuss school matters.

We know of one boy, scheduled to leave school, who was chosen for the track team. While he knew he was a fast runner, he did not realize he was of championship caliber. He did not become a drop-out, as he had planned, and, indeed, overnight found himself a hero to his fellow-students. It is interesting to observe that his academic work improved considerably. What better morale booster could possibly have been furnished?

On the way to our junior high school, we overheard two girls talking. One suggested that, inasmuch as it was a beautiful day, why not go to the park. The other said, "I can't. I have Sewing

Club today, and I have to finish my dress for the dance next week." This was really an immediate goal! With enough of this type of interest, how can such a program fail to be successful? (And, incidentally, what a favorable effect it had on attendance!) One of the authors found that on baseball club day, every child who belonged to the club generally came to school.

With competent leadership, newspapers, magazines, exhibits of all kinds, competitions, and also the performing arts, bring forth enthusiasm where even talent may be lacking. Children will come alive when working on such activities.

However, the extra-curricular activity program must have certain qualities if enthusiasm is to endure.

1) There must be freedom of choice. No child should be forced to partake in any activity he does not vountarily choose. This is not school! He must feel he is volunteering. The shy, timid, sensitive child should be encouraged graciously for he will often amaze you with his surprisingly creative accomplishments.

2) In a successful student activities program, children who may never have had a sense of responsibility should be helped to realize they are on their own—that what they do is up to them—and that

—*Official Photograph, Board of Education, City of New York*

FUTURE DESIGNERS IN THE EMBRYONIC STAGE

they are in a position to benefit themselves, to enjoy themselves, and to help others, too, to partake in this enjoyment.

EFFECTIVE USE OF LEISURE TIME

In these student activities, the children learn how to use their leisure time to advantage. This knowledge serves many purposes:

1) It precludes anti-social activities. The child who operates a "ham radio" does not steal cars. He finds enough excitement in talking to other operators thousands of miles away. It is a source of intellectual pride. We have a friend who continuously tells us, with delight, of the persons he has contacted in South Dakota, England, and France. The need for adventure, which might be the root of serious behavior problems, is here fulfilled by a transmitter.

2) One meets people with similar interests—and through them, other latent interests may be awakened. As a result of the contacts children make in these activities, they meet people with whom they can spend many happy hours and exchange ideas. Friendships are often nourished and maintained by a common interest children find in pursuing these activities. If a child has nothing to bring to a friendship it will not flourish. One of the most important goals of these activities is to awaken these interests, and encourage the children to share them with one another. How much more salutary this is than the rivalry that is often generated in the classroom!

3) The extra-curricular activities a child engages in may arm him with hobbies that will be invaluable in his later life. (How rich we adults are, who have many interests—the theatre, concert, golf, or gardening.) These activities contribute a great deal to physical and mental well-being, and make for a more contented, and a happier individual. Many hobbies may begin in early childhood.

FOSTERING FRIENDSHIPS BETWEEN CHILDREN
AND BETWEEN CHILDREN AND TEACHERS

Children develop friendships with others with whom they have common interests. They must, however, have the time and place to discuss these interests, and to establish common meeting grounds, to really get to know one another. This often happens when youngsters are working together on projects—newspapers, plays, in clubs. The classroom is surely a place for stressing social development; and, just as surely, the extra-curricular activities are even more so. The informality of the situation, the need for the leader to be aware of the social nature of the club, and the relaxed atmosphere all help to encourage the children to make friends.

We know of one man who made life-long friends working on

—Official Photograph, Board of Education, City of New York

EVERY CHILD A BORN ACTOR—GIVEN BUT HALF A CHANCE

his high school senior play. The cast and stage hands became so cohesive a group during the long hours of rehearsal, that they remained as a group long after.

A relationship between a child and his teacher often develops when the latter changes his role and emerges as a friend, or an associate. The distance established between child and teacher may be greatly diminished in these informal situations. They get a chance to talk to one another, and to enjoy one another's company. The extent to which a teacher can unbend, can relax and can enjoy working with young people will determine the extent to which he can establish friendships with them.

DEVELOPING LEADERSHIP QUALITIES IN BOYS AND GIRLS

A full student activities program can accomplish far more, to develop leadership, than the regular curriculum. In order to do so, however, the teacher or faculty advisor for the clubs, or the student government—or almost any of the other activities—must realize he is not, at this time, teaching. His is the act of guiding. The pupils must be given the opportunities to actually lead. If the adult establishes the situation so that the young people elect or choose a student leader—and if this leader then can direct the projects and the work of the organization, the young people are getting valuable leadership training. If, on the other hand, the adult is afraid to relinquish his power (and this is characteristic of many adults dealing with young people) the extra-curriculur activity is far too similar to a classroom teaching situation.

Children must be given responsibility, advised so that they can cope with it, and then permitted, encouraged and praised for handling it themselves. The boys and girls will work far more diligently for a peer than for an adult. This peer may need assistance from the faculty member, but it should be given "sotto voce" so that he does not lose status: Leadership training is extremely necessary if the student activities program in your school is to thrive.

INVOLVING CHILDREN IN THE STUDENT
ACTIVITIES PROGRAM

The full student activities program will, of necessity, involve many children. One of the by-products of this involvement is increased morale and school spirit. Boys and girls should be made aware of all of the opportunities available to them. The competitions with other schools—through the teams, cheerleaders and boosters, the trips and the clubs—all engender a good spirit. By giving each child a feeling of belonging, of being an important part of the school community, the morale of the individual is raised. We cannot make each child a basketball player or fan, but we can, by offering a variety of activities, find at least one activity for every child. Getting one for each, each boy or girl involved in his or her "thing," can do a great deal to improve the climate of the entire school.

When a new school opens, there are strong feelings of enthusiasm and, for a year or two, the school spirit remains high. After that, unless there is a constructive program, it sags. Our job is to supply the impetus, and this is most easily done through an extensive extra-curricular program.

DETERMINING THE NEEDS OF YOUR
SCHOOL'S CHILDREN

There are a number of aspects to be considered before you plan your program. By answering these questions, you can determine what is lacking in your school's student activities program:

1) Does your school have a representative government, whose members are elected by the students, and which actually represents them?

On every level of schooling, boys and girls should be able to have a voice in some of the decisions affecting them. This does not imply, in any manner whatsoever, that they dictate policy, but it does mean their opinions and wishes are taken into consideration —that their voices are heard.

2) Are your boys and girls learning democratic processes through class organizations? Do they elect officers who represent them when the general organization of the school convenes? Are they encouraged to discuss issues of importance to them as students in the school? Is this class government mandated by the school laws, or is it left to the discretion of the individual teacher? In many schools this aspect of the student activities program is not clearly defined, and the boys and girls lose out for this reason.

3) Do your children need a place for recreation and for social- izing? Are there an adequate number of parks, playgrounds and the like in your area? Do boys and girls go directly home after school, or do they spend their time in one another's homes?

In some areas, there is often no room for the children in their apartments, and they spend their time on the streets. We have seen children stay in the school building until it closes—with no particular activity going on—because it was a warm (physically as well as psychologically) place to stay.

4) Do many of your children need a place to study? Again, the crowded conditions in which some children live make this an absolute necessity.

5) Do the interests of large numbers of your students need to be expanded? We must confess this is a question which is almost impossible to answer in the negative, for we honestly believe every child should have the opportunity to get more from school than the regular curriculum offers.

6) Do your children need baby-sitting? Are their mothers em- ployed, so that they go home to empty houses?

7) Do your children have intellectual stimulation in their homes? We have found many, many areas where there is poverty of ideas, of regard for learning, of books and literature. Often we have seen not physical, but educational poverty.

8) Would your children benefit from having various types of teams—from being in competition with other schools? This does wonders for school spirit. It is part of adolescence to be involved with sports and teams, and these can lead to the happiest days of students' lives.

9) Are many of your children employed after school hours? In this case, you would have to plan some student activities during the school day.

10) Do you have many students who need tutorial help? Are your academic results below what you would like? In a situation where help is available, many children can be encouraged to seek it. (We feel this assistance must be sought. It cannot be compulsory —because if it is, it appears to the child to be an extension of the regular school day.)

11) Do you have good school morale and school spirit? Are your children happy to be part of your school? Are they willing to put themselves out for it? A full student activities program can raise spirit almost miraculously.

12) Are you anxious to have better rapport developed between students and teachers? Here, too, extra-curricular activities can work wonders because they place the student and the teacher in a non-classroom situation. Children who feel threatened in a

—Official Photograph, Board of Education, City of New York

YOUNG SINGERS IN UNISON DURING A SONG FEST

classroom, and there are many, automatically unbend in a club or after-school situation.

13) Can you count on the parents of your children to take an active part in a student activities program? (Working parents are difficult to involve. Parents who have a negative attitude are even more so. Yet parents can and should be involved if the program is to be an extensive one.)

14) Do you have funds available for this type of program or will it have to be self-supporting? Funding is almost always a problem, and often the limiting factor. However, we have seen funds raised to support football teams, magazines sold to pay for their publication, and candy sold to raise money for the school. It is wonderful, of course, to have unlimited funds, but even more wonderful to have a staff which will cooperate, parents who will assist, and children who will actively take part in fund raising.

This relatively simple list of questions will help you to determine the nature of your present extra-curricular program. By studying your answers, you can then proceed to further planning.

Personnel

We would suggest you survey your staff to determine the availability of personnel. Of necessity, an activities program is time-consuming, if conducted in the usual manner—after school. However, if you find that you cannot get enough teachers to run clubs, coach teams and the like, it is possible to schedule one or two periods per week during school hours as club periods, which are then conducted as if they met after school. This may be necessary if lack of funds is a severe problem or if you and your staff find it preferable.

One of the simplest ways to get the information you need is to distribute a survey form to every member of the staff—including auxiliary personnel such as the school nurse, the guidance counselors, the librarian, the administrators. It might read as follows:

We are contemplating the establishment of an extended student activities program. Will you please indicate below

1) Any clubs you are interested in running. These may be in the hobby area, in technical areas, in the arts.

2) Are there any teams you are capable of coaching, or would like to try?

3) Which days of the week are you able to stay until five o'clock?

4) Which afternoons are you available for tutoring?

5) Which evenings can you participate in the evening school?

We have funds available for some, but not all of these activities. We will try to distribute the positions equally, so that no one will be overly burdened, and so that every one participating will receive remuneration. (This, of course, will depend on circumstances within your particular school district.)

THE ACTIVITIES PROGRAM AND TEACHER BENEFITS

Very often there are teachers who are shy, sensitive, persons whose talents are not evident. Because they are retiring, they hesitate to volunteer. Yet, the perceptive principal will know wha' their talents are and suggest an activity which fits them. The teacher, himself, may be very much enriched spiritually, by dis covering he has more talent than he suspected. The morale booste is just as necessary for some teachers as for the children.

One of the authors was asked to obtain food for an institution for the aged. She took it on diffidently, fearful lest her activity be inadequate. To her surprise and delight, her success in the undertaking far exceeded her expectations. When she told her principal how surprised she was, at its tremendous success, he said he was not the least bit surprised. Both the principal and the teacher received delightful letters from the institution, and one of its administrators came to the school personally to express the institution's appreciation. Need I mention that the teacher held her head two inches higher?

Instead of working at other jobs after school (called, in some areas, "moonlighting") many teachers who need additional income to support their families, would be delighted to work with children in the student activities program. They will not have to travel to a second job, and they will be working with the same children— and the same supervisors.

Developing Rapport With Children

The informal situations set up in a student activities program provide opportunities for the children and teachers to work together in friendly, casual relationships, which foster the development of good rapport. Children do not feel tense or threatened, and can relax. They can get to know their teachers—and the teachers can get to know them. When they work together under such circumstances—clubs, teams or newspapers—the closeness and the empathy which develop help the teacher to work more effectively with that child in a classroom situation. The teacher-pupil relationship must remain, but co-existing with it is a people-to-people relationship, as well.

As each activity is suggested in subsequent chapters, you will find specific suggestions for staffing it. These will consider some of the psychology involved in bringing out leadership qualities in both your pupils and teachers.

School Government 2

In the last few years our young people have been very vocal in their demands for a "say" in the affairs of their schools. They ask to have their opinions considered, their voices heard. We believe they are right, that such demands are healthy, and constructive. We do not believe they are in a position to have absolute rule—to select teachers, or to establish curricula. This, we feel, would be an abdication on the part of the adults whose profession it is to administer the schools. However, by giving consideration to the opinions and to the comments of our boys and girls we and they are in a position to gain a great deal. Very often what they have to say has merit. If a textbook is poor, shouldn't they be able to call this to the attention of the administration? If they are not satisfied with the meals being offered for sale in the cafeteria, shouldn't they be able to do something about it? And by furnishing them with a forum, by establishing a system of elected officials to represent them, are we not giving them experiences in democratic living—which they must have if democracy is to succeed? At the same time, are we not also precluding rebellious acts which are detrimental to the welfare of both the teachers and the children? With this in mind, the following recommendations are given to help your school improve its student government.

INVOLVEMENT

The secret ingredients for success in every venture are the degree of involvement of its participants, and the wisdom of the decisions made. It is, indeed, difficult to infuse children with wisdom—but not with involvement. The wisdom should come, in large measure, from the faculty advisor, but the involvement must come from the boys and girls if the student government is going to succeed.

This involvement, this being a part of a group, is, as has previously been mentioned, extremely important for the psychological development of the child. He needs it—and the organization needs him. It is almost impossible, of course, to involve every child, but surely a large percentage can be induced to take part. Many methods for attaining this involvement will be found in the following pages; however—and make no mistake—these methods cannot be artificial or phony. They must be valuable projects, purposeful activities, if they are to cause children to really share in their student government.

When we use the term involvement, what do we mean? We use it to describe a state of intense interest—interest which ties or binds those who share it together. People involved in a project think about it, talk about it, work at it, often as a labor of love. Those who observed young people working in the Eugene McCarthy campaign of 1968 saw exactly the extent to which involvement can reach. In school situations this involvement can and must be striven for—although it is probable the intensity would not be the same.

As a result of involvement, the school spirit rises and rises. All of us have seen hundreds of students cheering their football team to victory; and there is a great deal to be said for this, for it is in large measure healthy and pleasurable for the young people. The spirit rises, too, within the school, as the activities of the student organization become more personal, more exciting—more involving.

G.O. VERSUS S.G.

Many schools have G.O.'s, the General Organization. Because we feel there is much to be gained from it, we suggest a name change. Rather than the ubiquitous G.O., call yours The _____
_____ Student Government, substituting the name of your

school for the _____ . (Even if the school is known as "#6," it is preferable to call it "The #6 Student Government." If the school is Midcity High School, then it would be The Midcity Student Government, or MSG.) The words "Student Government" will, we hope, indicate an active, representative student organization.

We suggest you use this device to stimulate interest. Have your students vote to determine whether or not they want this name change. Stress the fact that Student Government is an elected government, in which every youngster is urged to participate. Play it up! Have pupils with opposing opinions debate the issue in the auditorium. After the referendum, have the president announce the decision with great fanfare. Even if the boys and girls vote to keep the title of General Organization, they have made the decision.

Issuing membership cards and membership buttons with the legend _____ SG are good devices to motivate some of the pupils. Try to find items which are novel and interesting. You may wish to have a pupil design these, and even run a contest for them. We have seen fine results—in membership buttons, in particular—with interesting use of line and color. There is no need to limit the latter to the school colors either. A psychedelically colored and designed button can be far more fun.

You may wish to have the S.G. develop a motto or slogan. The pupils' creativity is again stimulated.

If there is a newspaper in your community which prints school news, have the student government secretary send an announcement of the issue, and the resultant action, to the editor. Your pupils and their parents enjoy seeing news of their school in print. Important events should be sent in—in advance, if possible, and written up completely, but briefly. Papers need material and your school, with its many students, can surely supply some. It may be decided to elect or appoint a Press Secretary for this purpose. His or her job, then, would be to prepare the press releases, working, of course, with a faculty advisor. *No reports should ever go out without being checked by this advisor, since the school is responsible for them.*

THE FACULTY ADVISOR OF THE
STUDENT GOVERNMENT

Choose a person for the task of SG advisor who needs an outlet —someone who is motivated and interested. Try to give him "free reign"—encourage him to experiment with activities and to stimulate the children. If he has drama and verve, he will convey this to them. If he is dull or unenthusiastic, unfortunately this, too, will probably be transmitted to the children.

For this leadership an individual is needed who loves to help young people become self-directing. He must throw out ideas, and then get the boys and girls to implement them. He must be able, too, to very diplomatically select those ideas suggested by the boys and girls which are feasible—and convert those which are not usable into possibilities. He is usually a young teacher, but not necessarily so. He may have had experience in student government, but this, too, is not essential. The most outstanding of his characteristics must be involvement, motivation, and drive, and the ability to enjoy working with children. These attributes are really, of course, those of an outstanding teacher.

HOLDING ELECTIONS

One of the most exciting aspects of the student government is the election of a staff of officers each year—usually in the month of June. Encourage participation by a large number of candidates. Make it possible for any child to run who gets the required number of signatures on his petition. We suggest you limit the number to run for each office to one per three hundred pupils. For example, if your school has a population of 1,800, there could be six candidates for president, six for vice president, etc. These would be the three boys and three girls per office who brought in the largest number of signatures by a specific date.

It is customary for the president to be a member of the graduating class, and for the vice president to be one class below. The secretary and treasurer should be one class below the vice president. For example, if a child is graduating in June, 1971, he would run for president in June, 1970. Your students may wish to run on tickets, which they would arrange themselves. Colors are very popular for this—the Blue Party, the Green Party, etc.

Each candidate should ask a classmate or another student to be his campaign manager. Encourage students to make posters and to give out buttons—or other forms of identification. (We've seen hair ribbons used very effectively.) Both candidate and manager should speak before every assembly—briefly, but, we hope, intelligently. If necessary there should be special assemblies for this purpose.

The campaigns should be carried on around real issues. Candidates should suggest plans for improving the school, for doing more for the students. Encourage original ideas, but be sure that all are checked first with the faculty advisor. "More dances and parties" is a very popular platform, but one which requires raising more financial backing. "A class day for every class," rather than just the seniors, "more clubs, intra-school teams" are typical issues —have the candidates look for those needs of the pupils which are not being fulfilled. Would they like a candy machine in the cafeteria, in the hall, or in the SG store? What would this mean in terms of littering the school? Should the school sponsor a field day or a picnic? Are there any serious problems within the school which might be improved? Is the school newspaper interesting? Are there recreational facilities such as playgrounds in the vicinity of the school? Does the school need to be beautified? How does the candidate propose to do this? Suggest to the candidates that they consult their friends and classmates for help in finding issues.

A special committee should be put in charge of the voting. Each class should have elected its class officers, and the vice president of the class should serve on this committee. It is his job to distribute ballots to every child in the class and to collect them after they are marked. Then a tally should be done in each class, working on the board, with the entire group participating. When the results are obtained, they should be sent down to the SG Office to be counted by the present year's officers. For example, Billy

Jones is running for the Presidency. He will be graduating in June, 1972. Therefore, he would run for President in June, 1971. If he were interested in the vice presidency, he would had to have run in June, 1970.

When the results are tabulated, the current President should announce the winners, and the results be published in the school newspaper. It should include human interest stories about each elected official and photographs.

The election of a Captain of the Monitorial Squad is an excellent idea—for this position is a very important one, and a boy who can be a good administrator is really needed. To balance this, you might have a girl elected as Captain of the Secretarial Squad. If these children are then trained as leaders, they can serve the school well, and they themselves will benefit from this valuable experience.

To hold a political convention, have a meeting of every SG representative, sometime in May. At this time, have each candidate be introduced by his campaign manager, and then make a short speech about himself. The representatives should decide whom they are going to support, and may wish to volunteer to serve as campaign workers. Unlike the national conventions, however, they should not decide who the candidates are to be. These are the boys and girls who have gotten the most signatures on their petitions.

Make the convention exciting. Representatives may come in "committed" to a candidate and applaud him, in the manner of national conventions, and may even carry banners. We would discourage more uproarious exhibitions, however.

Student Government Representatives must be elected at the time class elections take place, sometime in September or early October. We suggest two, with two alternates. (One boy and one girl on each.) The students should be made to realize these positions are extremely important—and choose all of their elected officials wisely.

The Student Government Assembly meets once every two weeks, and if it convenes during the school day, the representative (or, if he is absent, the alternate) must attend. This must be made clear to the teachers. It will be easier to avoid hard feelings if the

Assembly meets at different times, on different days, so that the students do not always miss the class which meets period 2 on Mondays, or period 6 on Thursdays.

TASKS OF THE STUDENT GOVERNMENT REPRESENTATIVES

The Student Government Assembly meets to suggest school rules, to vote on projects, activities, dances, trips, and other functions, and to act as a court with students who are law-breakers. It recommends actions to be taken to the principal.

Please note that the Assembly does not make laws, nor enforce them, but it does make suggestions and recommendations. However, if their suggestions are never taken, if the recommendations are rarely acted upon, the Student Government loses its significance. It will fail to hold the children's interests and ultimately become a nonentity. On the other hand, if the suggestions made by the students are not acceptable, it is wise to explain why and to suggest further work. Encourage them to continue to concentrate on the issues until recommendations are worked out in compromise, if necessary. These will probably be acceptable to the administration and to the children. Emphasize, always, that this is in observance of the democratic ideal.

STUDENT COURT

We suggest you experiment with a student court. We have found, however, that children are often too hard on each other—and a spirit of clemency should be emphasized.

You may wish to have the Student Government elect judges and have cases tried before them. If the verdicts are too severe, and in many cases they will be, there should be a Court of Appeals, which would have on it members of the faculty and of the student body.

The student court may be a very dramatic means of handling problems—and it often proves effective. Children care a great deal about the opinions of their peers, and are far less likely to resent punishment meted out. Be sure, however, that the "lawyers" have prepared their cases well, and that the judges are impartial. Having the Court of Appeals guarantees that any "injustice" can be corrected. However, if the court is consistently too lenient or too severe, the judges' decisions should be reviewed by the Court of Appeals. It is obvious that careful records must be kept in such proceedings.

As a by-product of this, children learn a great deal about the laws—and the way they function—by participating in a student court.

THE WORK OF THE ELECTED OFFICERS

The President of the Student Government is in charge of meeting and greeting the public. He must be present at all meetings of the Assembly and should report on these meetings to each grade once a month. He should edit the Student Government Newsletter, a one-page report of student activities published once every month, and given to each pupil.

It is his task to suggest projects and activities, to call for referendums when a vote from the students is necessary, and act as the intermediary between the students and the faculty. In this way he can present both sides of an issue.

He is in charge of Student Government dances and parties, and helps to draw up a calendar of events each month.

The Vice President presides over the Assembly Meetings, as the Vice President of the United States presides over the meetings of the United States Senate. He also takes the President's place, in the event of his temporary absence, assists him when necessary, and, should the President have to abdicate, the Vice President assumes the role of President.

He is also an assistant editor of the Student Government Newsletter. He may assist the President in acting as the intermediary between the faculty and the students.

The pupils should be encouraged to voice their ideas in school government by writing letters to either the President or the Vice

President. These should be discussed at the Assembly Meetings, and printed, with responses, in the Student Government Newsletter.

The Secretary of the Student Government keeps notes of all events and proceedings, helps with the duplication and distribution of the Student Government Newsletter. He is next in line to assume the Vice President's duties, if the Vice President must leave or is incapacitated. He does all correspondence for the Student Government.

The Treasurer is in charge of finances, including assisting in the operation of the Student Government Store.

He does the budgeting for parties, and other school affairs, and should be trained in the skills of buying and selling. He collects funds and is instrumental and actively involved in all fund-raising.

INTERESTING NEW STUDENTS IN SG

To engender interest in the Student Government, a great deal can be accomplished by sending the officers and members of the SG teams to speak to the students who will be entering the school. This is an excellent means of articulation and of smoothing the transition from one level to another. We have found this particularly successful when the boys and girls spoke for a short period of time, and then the floor was thrown open for questions. The questions, the audience was told, do not have to refer to the Student Government. They can be about anything the newcomers wish to learn. However, whetting the appetites of those entering is good, and allaying their fears even more so. Very often the school they are about to enter is considerably larger than the one they are used to, and the anxiety the children feel can be lessened by hearing boys and girls, not much older than themselves, talk about how much they enjoy their school. These speakers usually will do a glowing job. They should, of course, invite the boys and girls to join the Student Government, and tell them of all of the opportunities open to them. The faculty advisor should be on hand to answer questions the young people are unable to answer, but should not, at any point, take over the program. It should belong to the Student Government.

WORTHWHILE PROJECTS FOR STUDENT GOVERNMENT

There are a great many worthwhile projects which the Student Government can engage in. We will list some samples here.

Families in Need

In the philanthropic area, it is well to find out the needs of the immediate community. Determine which families or organizations need financial aid right in the vicinity of the school. Activities of this type must be conducted very deftly. Because of this need for deftness, far too often this important work is neglected. Encourage

THE NEEDY ARE NOT FORGOTTEN—
SOCIAL-MINDED STUDENTS AT WORK

the children to seek assistance for those families whom they know are in need.

When the immediate needs of the community have been ascertained and fulfilled, then the Student Government can move to other organizations. They may wish to send funds to the United Nations Children's Fund, or any other worthwhile philanthropic organization. Through the Foster Parent Plan they may decide to adopt a child. There are many, many organizations which would be most grateful for aid. By encouraging and permitting the children to contribute to philanthropic activities, we awaken their social conscience, which, we hope, will endure throughout their entire lives. Allow the children to suggest and vote for the cause for which they wish to work.

School Improvement

We can improve the school and its immediate surroundings by conducting campaigns for cleaning and beautifying the area.

Student Government can sponsor clean-ups of vacant lots, for example. We have a friend whose comment was, "My daughter leaves early each Saturday morning to help clean up the vacant lots. She gets up at seven o'clock without protest—which is, in itself, unusual—but you should see the room she leaves behind as she dashes out!"

For beautification, plants, bushes and trees can be planted around the school. If need be, planters can be made or purchased by the Student Government.

Electing a "Student of the Month"

Each month one student may be elected "Student of the Month" by the entire school. Sometimes the candidates should be those with the highest academic standings. Other months those who are most active in school affairs; still other times, those most helpful to their fellow-students. Another category might be the best athlete—or the best baseball or basketball player. Another might be an election for the best writer, painter, scientists, poet or actor or actress. Still another might involve the Best Groomed. These elections stimulate interest, and veer the children in the direction of self-improvement. Medals—loving cups or prizes should be awarded by the Student Government.

Electing a "Man of the Year"

Each year the Student Government may wish to select a celebrity for recognition. The person elected may visit the school, which makes for a great deal of excitement. (Be sure there is a photographer on hand, and notify the community newspaper.) The least he will do is respond with a letter, which may be prominently displayed.

Fund Raising

There are funds raised by the Student Government throughout the year. The dues and the profits from the Student Government Store are constant. However, we feel there should be one major project for fund raising since this provides the financial backing for many of the other projects.

We have run a candy sale over a week's time, with excellent results (see Chapter 12). Book Fairs, concerts, and shows can also be used. A flower or plant sale, a "white elephant" sale, or a sale of record albums are possibilities, as well. Professional photographers are often interested in taking and selling photographs of the students—with a significant share of the profit paid to the Student Government. Encourage the Student Government Assembly to discuss projects, and put this to a vote of all the students, since their involvement in the project will insure its success.

Invitations to Famous Persons

Many famous persons, particularly athletes, have responded to invitations written to them by the Secretary of the Student Government, culminating in their presence in our school. Real, live, vibrant experiences were shared by our children as they heard

CANDY SALE A WINNER

by Susan Horowitz

From November 30 to December 8 Junior High School 127's students and teachers have been participating in a candy sale. The goal of this drive was to raise funds for senior class activities. Looking at the results, it seems that almost everyone took part in the sale.

When the sale came to a close, there was one outstanding class which had contributed more money than any other. The class is 9-11 which will be lucky enough to receive a pizza party for its donations. Class 7SP1 and 8-3 sold the most candy in their grade and for this they will be getting a trophy.

As in most fund-raising drives, there is always one person in particular who stands out as being the one who contributed the most money and effort to the sale. Well, our school has such a person in 9-11. Rose Ann Truncale is the top student in 127; she sold $164 worth of candy. For giving so much money to the sale, she will have a choice of a tape recorder or a pair of radio sunglasses. We also have Mr. Perrino, who sold the most candy from among the teachers, totalling $119.

After hearing what the school had obtained from this drive, Mr. Evansohn said it was just "frantically wonderful." Last year the school had a magazine drive but it wasn't half the success that this turned out to be.

When this year's sale ended, the 9th year came out ahead with $4,761. Trailing behind them was the 8th grade with $3,750 and finally the 7th grade with $3,343. The total amount came to $11,834.

For the people who participated in the drive, certain prizes will be awarded. For instance, for those who sold 15 boxes, a mascot will be given; for the sale of 25 boxes, a snoopy dog, and for 50 boxes, you have a choice of either a guitar or transistor radio, a large mascot, camera set or free senior dues.

Thanks to everyone who participated, your seniors will be able to have the funds to carry on their activities.

—*Excerpt from Castle Hill Currents, Newspaper of Junior High School 127, Bronx, New York*

Althea Gibson, Jim Bouton and even the Baseball Hall of Fame member, Roy Campanella, speak to them.

We suggest you have your Secretary write to persons whom your children would enjoy meeting, thus making your school a very exciting place, and encouraging the kind of hero worship which benefits the children. At this time, too, have a photographer on hand, and notify the newspapers.

Dances

The Student Government sponsors a number of dances through-out the school year. There should be large dances, open to the entire school, and smaller ones for different grades. Surely it is the task of the Student Government to help bring the children closer together, and to encourage warm friendships.

We have found that if a dance has motif, it is easier to decorate for it and to advertise it. Each holiday can be used for this purpose.

Dances may be used, if you wish, to raise funds for worthwhile causes, or the needs of the school. However, there should be a number of affairs where there is no charge.

Faculty advisors or parents, or both, must be present during any school function to insure safety.

To encourage the boys to dance we suggest a "Sadie Hawkins' Day" occasionally when the girls may invite the boys, and ask them to dance.

Parties

We believe the Student Government should sponsor several parties during the course of the school year. This differs from a dance in that refreshments are served. You may wish to use some of these ideas:

a) A Welcome Back to School Party in September.

b) A Halloween Party—Encourage originality by making this a costume party and by giving prizes for the best costumes. You can also have a Pumpkin Contest—Each child is invited to bring in a pumpkin he has decorated, prizes being given for the most original. Select a theme for the costumes—such as Wild West, Gay Nineties, or Inanimate Objects. (The latter is great fun, re-quiring a good deal of ingenuity.)

c) An Easter Bonnet Party—prizes for the fanciest hats—con-structed to indicate the name of a song.

These are a few ideas. The boys and girls will have many, many more—ranging from light shows to circus extravaganzas. We believe parties should not be used to raise funds—unless it is absolutely necessary. The refreshments may be as simple or elaborate as the budget dictates. Allow the Student Government to decide—after the Treasurer presents the situation to them.

"Senior Doings"

As seniors, boys and girls expect and seek recognition from the Student Government. There are a number of ways to give them this reward. They may wear Senior Hats supplied by the Student Government (if the treasury can afford them). They may be given a special senior trip. On one designated day, it is fun to allow the pupils to "take over" the school. A pupil should teach every senior class, and the Student Government President replace the principal. On that day the seniors may be permitted to wear special costumes. Allow them to select their own theme and have a dance that afternoon to further commemorate it. Many adults we know still remember their High School Senior Days clearly. One friend tells of her quest for an unusual costume. She kept asking her family, "What shall I go as? What shall I go as?" Finally, in sheer desperation, her sister said, "Go as a Bloomin' Idiot." She did—flower pot on her head, flowers out of her ears. And she won the first prize, too, for originality! Help the Student Government make this the day your seniors long remember.

Parents Day

The Student Government may decide to have a specific day when they invite all parents to visit the school. Unlike the Open School Week, when the school is opened by the Board of Education, this day should come from the children. They should plan the events, making sure there are some which are exciting. They may wish to serve refreshments, or even lunch. The President of the Student Government would greet the parents, and each officer might speak, discussing the work of the students through the Student Government. The parents should be shown the projects which are completed, and those which are in the offing. Then they should be taken on a tour of the building by the Student Government Representatives. A show of some kind should follow.

If an entire day's program would be too time-consuming, the parents might be invited to a "Coffee Klatch" or to a "Tea" by the boys and girls through their organizations. The same greetings, short speeches and tours should follow. Actually a two-hour program would be adequate, from 1:00 to 3:00 in the afternoon.

This plan has much to be said for it. Parents want to see what is going on and love being invited out. We recommend it be suggested to your Student Government Assembly for voting on it.

Should they decide to experiment with it, please be sure the notices go home—that the children do not put them into their notebooks and forget about them. Perhaps it would be wise to use a tear-off slip, which each child would have to return, signed. In this way, the Planning Committee, set up by the President, would know how many guests were expected.

OPINION POLLS

Another method to involve all of the boys and girls in the school in decision making is through the medium of opinion polls. In matters concerning dress, for example, it is logical to poll the entire student body for their feelings. We recall an incident in regard to the wearing of ties. The representatives voted to retain the rule stating a boy had to wear a tie every day that he came to school. The student body disagreed, and made it rather obvious, by disregarding it.

In matters of dress, since styles change so rapidly, restatements of position are important. It is imperative, however, that the administration go along with the majority opinion. Each issue should be considered before it is put before the students, and the possible outcomes considered. If the administration is not prepared to abide by the decision, then do not put the issue to a vote. We have in mind the long hair the boys are wearing in many parts of the world today. If the pupils want it, can the administration tolerate it? Many times there are fads which move along quickly. One example of this was the Indian-style headband some of the young ladies decided to wear. This came and went in a very short period of time. The wearing of blue jeans, however, has been more enduring, possibly because they meet a need. They are inexpensive, easy to launder (this is not to say they are laundered, very often) and the older they get, the more fashionable they are.

The area of clothing is a very important one to the young people, and can be an important issue—of divisiveness or of solidarity. I have heard girls say, with great pride, "In my school we can wear slacks to class." This, we know, is not permissible in many, many schools, and yet we confess to believing they are far more modest than mini-skirts. Students will fight for the right to dress in the manner in which they wish—freedom of dress, if you will. Once the freedom is granted, the issue loses its steam. The same young lady we quoted above added, "I can't understand why the girls don't wear them so much any more."

This is one area in which the little issues become big ones—the molehills become mountains. Forbid shorts or slacks to high school students, and a mountain is created. Permit them, and it is a nothing. We submit that the antagonism created in the minds of the children when we flatly forbid them to do something in the context of dress is hardly worthwhile. We believe our authority should be saved for the important issues.

TOWN HALL MEETINGS

Probably one of the most important projects for the Student Government is the "Town Hall" meeting to be held periodically, at which boys and girls are able to state their problems and air their grievances. Allow the Student Government to decide how often and when to hold these. To insure an active student body, request the presence of the Student Government Assembly members—the representatives, and the officers.

We suggest you ask that questions be submitted before the meeting so that duplicates may be eliminated. Then, have the Secretary read the question, and the *students* present suggest solutions.

It is most important that the questions be discussed and answered by boys and girls whenever possible. This airing of grievances is not as profitable if it becomes a debate between pupils and teachers. If a peer can talk over the situation, give his views of it, and even give advice, his schoolmates are far more likely to accept what is said.

At times the faculty adviser may be called upon to answer, and at others it may be necessary to table the question until the next meeting. This should not happen too often, however.

A full record should be kept of the questions and discussions, and should be read by all the members of the administration. It may even be worthwhile to tape record it—if this does not inhibit the boys and girls.

Questions not submitted in writing should be discussed, too. The President of the Student Government, or the Vice President, should be the Chairman. Orderly, intelligent freedom of speech should be fostered. Pupils should be made aware of certain ground rules. For example, personalities cannot be discussed. No one can get up and say, "Miss X can't teach." If he wishes to, a person can say, "I'm having trouble with my French grammar," and he will be told how and when he can get help. However, we've heard complaints about the temperature in rooms, the dirt in the desks, and money disappearing from coat pockets. These things could be remedied. Be sure that no child is ever penalized for his comments at a Town Hall Meeting.

Questions and grievances may be submitted at any time to the President or Vice President. They may decide to call a meeting when a number of these complaints have been received.

CONCLUSION

The Student Government is one of the most important aspects of a full, vital student activities program. The key to its success is involvement, and the amount of involvement is a measure of its success. Pupils become involved through the Student Government elections, through projects, through fund-raising, through dances and parties, through the medium of Student Government Assembly where decisions are made by representatives, through opinion polls and through the Town Hall forum where their grievances are heard, and their questions answered.

Eleanor Roosevelt once said she would rather light a candle than curse the darkness. In encouraging our children to actively participate in Student Government, we are permitting them to "light the candle," to do something constructive to improve their school—and to act upon them if they have complaints. How often today are students themselves cursing the darkness and cursing their previous inability to act!

No less a poet than William Wordsworth said that the "child is father to the man." This great thinker spoke of the child as "thou sole philosopher." Let us then encourage our young philosophers to participate actively in the government of their schools, bringing their fresh thoughts to supplement and vitalize ours.

Class Organization   **3**
and Class Government

In our country, we have both federal and local government. So, too, in our school situation should we have both. The school Student Government is fully described in the previous chapter. In the present one we shall outline plans for *class government* or *class organization*. Custom has decreed the use of the terms Class President, Vice President, etc. and we feel this has merit. Practicing democracy is a must in the classroom—democracy in this sense being defined as representative government, accompanied by both rights and responsibilities. We see little value in establishing a class or school government which does not function. If the students are not given the opportunity to live up to their responsibilities and benefit from their rights, there is no point in having class officers or a class organization.

Before we begin, let us state certain basic principles. There is one person who is the figure of authority and who must be in control of the class at all times. This is the teacher. He may delegate authority; he may extend courtesies; he will, we are sure, observe the students' rights, but he never gives up—for even one minute—his mastery of the situation. The reason for this is clear. In the classroom, chaos is to be avoided—and a chaotic condition can result from the absence of the teacher. However, his presence, it is hoped, is enough for him to maintain a relatively calm atmosphere. We are not referring to absolute silence. We surely do not mean he cannot allow the Class President to take over completely. On the contrary, we are most anxious for him to structure this. But, behind all activities, he must be there, guiding the youngsters quietly and efficiently. Of course, there are occasions when the teacher will not be present in the room, and when the President will "take over." If the teacher has had the class under control, there will be no problem. If the teacher's discipline has been poor, the President will have difficulty.

Teaching democracy is not simple—it involves a great deal of skill—but we must teach it, and we can, with benefits to both students and teachers.

BEFORE THE ELECTIONS

Decide at the beginning of the year, with your children, how many different sets of officers they think they should have—how often they would like to hold elections. We believe that every ten weeks is about the shortest period of time anyone should serve, but that three or even two times a year is possible. Decide at this time, too, how often a person may be re-elected—whether he can succeed himself more than once. Make sure that the method of electing is also worked out carefully, and in advance. We would suggest that a secret ballot be used. While this is more cumbersome, it is also a better way because it guards against hurting the feelings of any of the children. Boys and girls can be inordinately sensitive and, rather than risk hurting even one, we should protect them. It is one thing to not be elected, and quite another to be told that Joey voted against you! The actual work of unfolding the ballots and counting them is a task for the present set of officers, so that after the first elections, they present no extra work for the teacher at all.

We would suggest that six officials be elected at each designated date—the Class President, Vice President, Secretary and Treasurer, and two Representatives to the Student Government Assembly. Two alternates should be chosen, in case the representatives are unable to attend meetings, for their tasks are very important ones in an active Student Government. Should any officer leave office, everyone moves up one notch—so that if the Secretary moves away, the Treasurer takes over his job, and the first alternate chosen becomes the regular representative.

Before anyone is nominated or elected, the tasks of the officers should be carefully and completely delineated. Start with the office of Student Government Representative. Ask the boys and girls to suggest what his work will be. Obviously he will have to attend meetings of the Student Government Assembly, and vote on the numerous issues presented to that group. Point out that the boys and girls in the class should have the opportunity to instruct their representatives in how to vote—as we try, by writing to our Congressmen and Senators, to inform them of our feelings before they vote in their respective houses. The representatives will suggest issues as well as vote on them, and here, too, they may be instructed by their classmates. Alternates must be elected as well. It is possible to have a child serve as an alternate, and as another officer, although this, too, should be decided in advance. Stress the importance of the role of the representative.

The President of the class acts in place of the teacher when the teacher is not present and assists the teacher when asked to do so. During fire drills he takes his place at the beginning of the line and leads the class out. He must be respected by the children for his ability and must be given the prestige due the office. He will attend meetings of the Class Presidents, when they are called, and he will preside when class meetings are necessary. He will lead the class in setting up class projects, in operating projects sponsored by the Student Government of the school, and in giving class parties. While on trips, he is in charge of the decorum, and will speak to any children who are misbehaving. He must be able to set himself apart—to be on the side of administration, and yet to remain a friend of the members of the class, so that they will feel free to come to him with grievances.

Outline the role of every officer before he is elected, so that the children know what will be expected of him, and so that their classmates are able to choose wisely.

The Vice President takes over the duties of the President if the latter is absent, and is, in addition, a key person at fire drills, where he takes his station in the middle of the line. He is also the elected monitor, running any errands for the teachers. He is the person to go to for assistance, should any emergency take place, while the President is in charge of the class. The Vice President will notify the office of the absence of a teacher, for example. The Vice President is also responsible for checking to see that the clothing closets are locked when the class leaves the room.

The Secretary does the clerical work of the class, keeping track of the homework assignments, for example. It is also his job to telephone every child who is absent, to give him the assignments. This is an extremely important task, and one which makes the requirement for the job a point to be stressed. Should a child not own a telephone, make it possible for him to telephone from the school office. It is also the Secretary's job to write any and all letters from the class, and to send invitations to speakers or parents when necessary.

The Treasurer collects the Student Government dues, and all other monies, and is responsible for record keeping. In addition to this, he takes the attendance, daily, writing it on the blackboard in a corner of the room. He also lists the pupils who are absent and those who came in late. His is the task of making collections for philanthropies and of administering fund-raising projects when run by the Student Government.

HOLDING ELECTIONS

Nominations should be made from the entire class and, if seconded and accepted, the pupil's name should be placed on the board. Start with the office of Representative, and elect one boy and one girl. Decide with the class, beforehand, how many candidates should be placed in nomination (above six the number becomes too unwieldy). After six pupils have been nominated, give out small sheets of paper, and have the children write the words "Student Government Representative" on the paper and write in one name from among the boys nominated. After this is done, collect the sheets and hand them to one person to tally. Next, do the same for the girl Representative. Continue with the other officers, working up to the Presidency. We have found this method adds to the excitement of the elections. For the second time around, hand the votes to the officer currently holding the job, for counting.

When the officers have been elected, place their names on a

corner of the board, over the class designation. The first task of the Secretary is to prepare a chart, with this information and the date of their election. This should be made as attractive as possible and kept on view, even after the officers have been re-elected.

Every child in the class should have the opportunity to be elected to class office, and for this reason there should be no requirements or restrictions placed on the nominations. Quite often you will find boys and girls placed on the ballot who are discipline problems. It is possible that service as a class officer may prevent their getting into trouble, and the chance to serve should surely not be denied to them. We all know of children whose cause of misbehavior is the need for attention—and who have not been able to get it any other way. Perhaps by being elected, and having the prestige of the title of a class office, such behavior can be averted. This is not always true, but quite often will work out in this way.

Holding Elections Four Times a Year

We feel that each child who gets the opportunity to serve will benefit from it sufficiently to warrant changing your class officers four times a year. There must be a rule, however, establishing the number of times a youngster may hold the office, and how many times he may succeed himself, or the entire process can lose its value. Serving as a class officer can elevate the child's opinion of himself—and for many children this is essential. With six officers, and a rotation of four times a year, almost every child can get the chance to function in one capacity or another. Furthermore, this service should appear on the child's permanent record for future reference. This may be just the boost this child needs, to bolster his self-image and raise his sights. It is particularly valuable for the retiring, shy child, and although he is not usually the one chosen for nomination, he surely has a chance.

STUDENT AWARENESS OF RESPONSIBILITIES

If we are to use the class organization and the Student Government as teaching tools, to give our children experiences in democracy, and in the functioning of the democratic way, we must make them aware of the processes going on. We do this first by outlining the tasks of the officers, before they are elected. We next must give them the situations in which they function. If the President is a mere figurehead, or the teacher's "Yes-man," little of worth will be learned. If, on the other hand, he actually functions—does things for and with the pupils—the entire concept of democracy can grow in the children's minds. Let us say there is a drive to raise money for the American Red Cross. In many classrooms the teacher announces, "This is Red Cross Week," speaks a bit about how valuable the organization is, and then asks the children to bring in contributions. Consider how differently this may be handled. The teacher asks the President to appoint a committee of pupils to study the work of the Red Cross, to telephone the local branch, to get as much material as possible, and possibly to ask for a speaker to come in to discuss his work. (This must be done quickly or it loses its flavor—we have discovered that a sense of urgency is far better than a long, stretched out period of activity.)

After this is done, the President reports back to the class. "This is the work the American Red Cross has been doing," he begins. He then goes on to describe it in detail. He follows this by saying, "We have been asked to raise some money. How do you suggest we go about this?" The boys and girls make suggestions. The President is, of course, chairing this meeting, and the Secretary taking notes. The class comes to a decision—possibly by popular accord, possibly by voting on it—and then the President proceeds to appoint chairmen, and to get the class to work.

In times of national and international disasters, our young people have worked, with their parents, to help alleviate suffering, and save lives. For example, when hurricanes strike our shores, it is often the boys and girls who work around the clock helping to supply food and clothing, caring for babies, and notifying friends and relatives of people in trouble. This stems in part from a familiarity with the work of the Red Cross, which should be developed in the classroom, not by the teacher, but by the class officers. If it is done in this way, the pupils are far more receptive than if they are told to participate, or are ordered to do so.

At the untimely death of Dr. Tom Dooley, one of the authors

—*American Red Cross Photo by John Hendrickson*

GULFPORT, MISSISSIPPI, AUGUST 26, 1969

Red Cross youth volunteers work on telegram inquiries at Red Cross disaster headquarters concerning relatives, friends and property in the area affected by hurricane Camille. Right to left are Jo Ann Puckett, Bruce Grant, Audrey Grayson, and Gladys Tart.

was teaching a class which had been rather lethargic. The case was discussed, in much the manner outlined above, and the imagination of the children caught. They worked on a series of projects, from shining shoes—which they volunteered to do—to selling cake in the school cafeteria. They were tremendously proud of making a significant contribution to the organization which was established to carry on Dr. Dooley's work.

It is the children's responsibility (and they should be taught this) to bring any complaints to the Student Government Representatives, if they refer to schoolwide laws and procedures, or to the class officers, if they refer to problems within the class. It is also their responsibility to choose their officers wisely, for these are the people who will serve them. Discuss with the children the concepts of national and local elections—that one votes for the person whom one considers to be the best for the job, not one who is a friend or acquaintance, or who is a "nice guy." One should never vote for a person who has intimidated him, as sometimes may happen in a classroom situation. This should be discussed, frankly and openly. If fear is permitted to enter the picture, the validity of the democratic process is lost. For this reason, a secret ballot should always be used.

Above all, we must teach our children to cooperate with their elected officers, to participate in programs they are running, and to back them when necessary.

Voting is both a right and a responsibility—this concept is essential to their understanding of government. We are aware of the large number of persons who do not cast their ballots for extremely poor reasons (such as a rainy day). We should show how wrong this is, so that children are able to project this from their classroom to the local and national situation.

Freedom must be taught as *freedom under law*—that a person is not free to harm another, that he is free, but that he must also obey laws and regulations. Children, we have found, do not always fully comprehend this, and there is a transfer of this to their adult lives.

The Class Supreme Court

You may wish to allow your children to experiment with a court, in which they try their classmates for infringement of class rules. As we discussed in the Student Government Court, this may cause problems, because the youngsters tend to be more severe in punishment than adults would be. However, this method offers possible solutions for recurring problems. There are children who frequently are disruptive, and merely discussing their behavior may not be sufficient to prevent its recurrence. The court may be able to adopt a stronger, but still fair policy. These measures are worth taking before the administration must act, and should be carefully considered by the children. The teacher must be aware, too, of what steps can be taken, so that the boys and girls are not "whistling in the dark" when they ask for a child to be removed from their class for constant disruptive behavior.

BUILDING THE PRESTIGE OF THE CLASS

Discuss with the boys and girls the concept of self-government in terms of the effect it has on them—and on others with whom they come into contact. If the children can control themselves, the teacher is able to give the best possible lessons of which he is capable. Not only this, but the class develops a reputation of being a good one, and is included in outings, and in other activities from which it might be omitted if it had a bad name.

The prestige of every class can be enhanced by contributing to the activities of the school. In philanthropic work, for example, they can raise the most funds, or offer the most time and effort. Boys and girls can be made to realize they are working for the common good, but that this reflects on them, as well. They learn as they work, too, to help others and to build their own characters.

DEVELOPING SELF-DIRECTION AND SELF-DISCIPLINE

One of the greatest benefits to be derived from an active class organization is the development of self-discipline and self-direction in the youngsters. Once these are developed teaching them is a joy. We are only too well aware of how much energy many teachers must spend in maintaining discipline. It uses up far too large a portion of their time, and this is consequently removed from the time they would spend teaching. By helping your children to take care of themselves, you gain extra help in the classroom. However, if a teacher is weak, the class organization will probably reflect this. The President, in large measure, represents the figure of authority, the teacher. Therefore, as class decisions are made, and as the elections are held, the concept must be stressed that all is carried out in an orderly fashion (indeed, this must be the keynote—freedom with responsibility). No "fooling around" should be accepted. The program must start out seriously, and be carried through in this manner. Children must take it in this spirit if it is to succeed.

CLASS PROJECTS

We believe that the more projects a class is involved in, the less difficulty there will be with discipline and with other problems. The following are some in which your class may wish to engage. It is important, though, that the children feel they are initiating them themselves:

Making Items for People in Hospitals

There are many items which may be made, either in industrial arts or home economics classes which shut-ins would appreciate. Tissue holders, magazine stands, waste baskets, eyeglass cases are but a few. If these are made before the Christmas holidays, they spread cheer to the recipients as well as the doers.

Repairing Toys

Many, many children have toys in broken or incomplete condition, which can be repaired, and used by other youngsters. In some cities, if these toys are collected and given to the Police and Fire Departments, they repair them and distribute them. Your class may wish to do the collection, the repair and even the distribution themselves.

Collecting Newspapers

Old newspapers are worth money. Your children can collect these, and sell them. In some areas, if the children's visits are preceded by a telephone call, the results are better—for people will often save the papers if they know they will be collected.

Writing to People in Hospitals

Letters can be very important to shut-ins, and your children may wish to embark on a letter writing crusade. Their letters will be welcomed wherever they are received, whether in Veteran's Hospitals or Old-Age Homes.

Visiting and Entertaining at Nursing Homes

Singing songs, putting on plays, playing records, or playing cards are some of the ways that young people can help others. How does one explain to children that their youth and vitality are so good for older folks—that a visit is like sunshine?

Neighborhood Clean-Up Campaigns

Drives such as clean-up campaigns may be carried on by classes, as well as the entire school. Making a street or neighborhood, which was once a mess, into an attractive area is surely a worthwhile project, and one which gets the children working out in the fresh air. They become aware, too, of the amount of work involved in the removal of litter. One newspaper, for example, can cover ten square feet of ground, making it look filthy.

Collecting Out-Grown Clothing

Unfortunately there are areas of our country where children are unable to go to school because they do not have clothing or shoes. Yet many, many usable items are discarded because of the lack of anything better to do with them. Your children may collect such clothes. There is usually a drive made by Roy Rogers and Dale Evans which deserves their support. The children may be encouraged to go from house to house collecting. This should be done in groups of three or four, however, rather than alone, particularly if the children are young. Even torn or worn clothing is of value, for it can be sold as rags, but all materials should have been washed before collection. A notice sent out by the teacher, before the collection, advising this, is essential.

Collecting Magazines

Old magazines should not be permitted to die, for there are many who would enjoy reading them. Your children can collect these and give them to an organization or hospital.

Planting Trees and Shrubs

If your area is one in which trees can be planted, your children may start them from very small plants. It is fascinating to watch these grow—particularly such trees as the mimosa or the weeping willow, which grow very, very quickly. Shrubs, too, are interesting to watch develop, and flowering ones particularly so.

The projects we have listed are for all ages, depending on your youngsters. The more sophisticated the children, the more difficult it is to select appealing work, but it can be done, nevertheless, and is well worth the time and effort.

Collecting Money for UNICEF

One simple endeavor for little ones, and with very much to be gained, is the collection of money for the United Nations Children's Fund. At Halloween time they can get special containers. At the same time your teachers can work with them on the concept of poverty in the world. Fighting hunger, or doing any other work to help their fellow men, no matter where they live, what their race or color is most worthwhile. It is a lesson every child needs!

DEVELOPING LEADERSHIP

A program of class government will not work unless your teachers work with the students to develop their leadership qualities. This is done by having the teacher meet with the officers, and asking them what they think their roles are. Then he should discuss each aspect of the role, so that the youngster is sure of what is expected of him. The teacher will then discuss these duties with the class, stressing the fact that the officers *must* do them— that they have no choice. If, while the teacher is out, the President has trouble with a child, the child knows that trouble must be discussed with the teacher. The goal is to prevent it from occurring again.

Teach the President to act as chairman at meetings, and to offer some suggestions himself—to start the intellectual ball rolling. Make sure the rest of the class understands the exact way in which each officer will do his job, so that no one feels he is being "unfair" by doing it. Make it seem wrong, if you can, not to do it—because it is wrong if the entire group is being annoyed, for example, by one child who refuses to do his part by cooperating. In a fire drill, for instance, every single person is relied upon to be quick and quiet, but if there are youngsters who are not, it is the task of the President and Vice President to try to improve upon the situation. If they cannot, then the teacher must step in.

Encourage the boys and girls to be outspoken—to give vent to their feelings and their emotions, but to do so in the right place and at the right time. The frustration a youngster can feel, if he never gets a chance to make himself heard, can hinder his development. He gets to feel: "What's the use? I can't do anything about it, anyway." Get him to open up, to voice his feelings. Perhaps his will be the voice others will rally around.

At the same time, make sure the youngsters perceive their responsibilities as citizens. There is far more to this than merely complaining, and they must be aware of this. If they see a child steal, or hit someone, they must report it—to the teacher, preferably—but this is their responsibility as a citizen, and a most important aspect of it. If they see injustice of any sort, try to encourage them to speak up against it. If they never do, how will they know how to behave as adults?

CLASS DAY

We believe that one day a year should be a really hilarious day, one to make the children happy. We suggest you ask the youngsters how they would like to celebrate it—perhaps by a party in school, a trip to a park for a picnic and games, a trip to a theatre to see a play, or a costume party all day. Consider their suggestions, take a vote on it—but have it! Make this one of the rewards for the activities of the class organization. Particularly if the class has engaged in worthwhile projects, they should be rewarded; but even if they have not, this can be a wonderful way to establish rapport, and to make the next year's class organization something to work hard for.

CONCLUSION

One little eighth grader, a girl, was elected class President. She stood up and requested silence, rather timidly. No response. She spoke a little louder. Still the din continued. Finally, she shouted, above the voices, "Q-U-I-E-T!" and that did it. The boys and girls looked at her expectantly. She smiled and said, "I thought you elected me President. I didn't think I was going to have to be a teacher."

All of us realize that the roles are similar, and yet different. By fostering the existence of an active class government, we build up in the children's minds the differences between the two. Far too often, teachers tell boys and girls what to do. There is little decision making. The class government forces them to make decisions. The teacher is the figure of authority, but with the class government, the authority figure is *elected*—is actually selected by the children themselves. Within this framework they help to make the rules which govern their behavior, and to assume responsibility for their actions. They are given the opportunities they need to set up their own projects. There is a forum for them to air their grievances. With all of these devices, we are training our young people to live and function in a democracy. We hope this will help them to think problems through, rather than "letting George do it." It is essential that our young people know exactly what their form of government is—and they will know it best by living it.

Determining Which Clubs 4
Your Students Want—
and Making Them Succeed

The *club program* is one of our most ingenious devices, for it enables us to accomplish several things at the same time. It is a teaching device without the formality of the classroom situation. It is motivated by the children's interest, and consequently topics can be selected in accordance with the needs and wishes of the boys and girls. It works without a curriculum (indeed the curriculum is structured by the pupils themselves, so that they get from the club those things which they want and need). This, in itself, is an educational incentive. Clubs should definitely be part of your student activities program.

Before establishing the club program in your school, you will need certain information:

1. It is necessary to poll the members of your faculty to determine which clubs they are qualified to conduct, and which they would care to run. It is possible that the two do not always coincide. A faculty member may be interested in skiing, but not be an experienced skier—and the question is whether he is qualified to run a club. In terms of skiing, the answer might be no, but in terms of other clubs (such as coin-collecting), there is no reason why a person could not be a relative novice, and still manage to run a club quite effectively. However, there should never be an attempt to fool the boys and girls. The leader should tell them he, too, is learning along with them.

2. You will need to determine how much funding is available,

for this may determine when the clubs will meet. Consider the following: clubs may meet during school hours, if there are problems in paying the teachers for extra time. This device may also prove valuable because, if there are many boys and girls who work after school, they cannot attend club meetings; but they could if the clubs are held during school hours. Children who travel by school bus would have to participate in clubs which convene during school hours, and this must be taken into consideration in your planning.

We do prefer a club program which lasts from one and one-half to two hours after school. The children are more relaxed after school, and the tension of the day disappears. There are also many youngsters who need the school as a refuge; it can be a place for study and contemplation as well as for club meetings. It affords opportunities for the boys and girls to socialize and to make new friends as well.

Let us start by listing some of the clubs you may wish to establish in your school. We are sure that you will not attempt to have all of these, but the following is a basis for your consideration.

We suggest you then survey your children, telling them to indicate their preferences. Be sure to inform them that not every club is feasible (because there may not be leaders available) but that, if the demand is great enough, every attempt will be made to find a capable and suitable person who will be willing to assume the responsibility.

We have categorized many of the clubs according to subject areas, and listed them in this manner for purposes of organization only.

SUGGESTED SCIENCE-ORIENTED CLUBS

Aeronautics

Geared to those children whose interests lie in this direction, a club may be a fascinating experience. They can do experiments pertaining to aircraft structure and study aerodynamics. They may be taken to aircraft companies, to factories manufacturing planes, and to airports. Visiting the control tower, if this is possible to arrange, is exciting as well as educational; however, even standing on the observation decks of most large airports provides a thrill.

Various museums have fine exhibits related to this study. If feasible, you might even arrange for rides in jets, particularly thrilling for those children who have never flown. (Parental permission is absolutely essential, of course.)

"Ham Radio" Operation

It is indeed fascinating to speak to people half-way around the world, and this is done frequently by amateur radio buffs. If your school can afford to set up a station, this may be a source of interest to the children which can remain with them long after they reach adulthood. It can spark the scientific talent that is so often dormant in many young boys. What interest could possibly broaden a child more than one which enables him to speak to another person thousands of miles away—where customs and ways of life are entirely different from ours? Is this not an effective means of drawing people together from all parts of the earth? The world becomes smaller and our understandings and sympathies larger. All this may be generated in a club which initiates this kind of activity.

You will need an advisor who has a license and can teach the International Morse Code. Setting up the system can be a very interesting part of the project and one in which the entire club may take part. This, too, would help the children if they wished to set up their own equipment at home.

Science Experiments

Youngsters love experimentation, and a club based on this can be a huge success, particularly if it is the children who do the experiments. There are a vast number of possible experiments, and the leader will find that the youngsters, if encouraged to do so, will bring in many more suggestions.

Try to include all areas of science in this club. Chemistry is a natural, of course, but biology, physics and earth science should surely be included. It is necessary, too, to find new experiments, rather than repeat those done in the science classes. However, outstanding or particularly interesting experiments, or those done as demonstrations by the teacher, may be repeated by the youngsters.

Astronomy

Since man appeared on earth, he has gazed at the stars in awe. With several telescopes, and people interested in the science, astronomy becomes the subject for a fascinating club and hobby. Studying the stars and the moon can be done right in one's own backyard. Nature often offers us phenomena such as eclipses and shooting stars which the boys and girls enjoy tremendously, and visits to museums and to planetariums are valuable additions. They, too, are the source of information. Since time immemorial, astronomy has intrigued the fancy of the scientist, the poet and the layman, too.

Oceanography

One of the newest and most fascinating fields of science can be found, if one lives on the coast, right on one's own seashore. The study of the sea, and of the riches it offers, with the possibility of scuba diving and the use of glass bottom boats, makes for a wonderful club program. This should be approached from many viewpoints. How can the sea be made to feed the billions of people who inhabit the earth? How can underwater oil be located? And the age-old question—how deep is the ocean, and what is its topography? Is there really a missing continent—Atlantis? All of these are bound to stir the imagination of the boys and girls. Films can be obtained, and speakers and lecturers will enrich the club, as well as field trips by the score.

Geology

Another science, encompassing far more than the identification of rocks, is geology, which offers fascinating areas for study in a club situation. Field trips are particularly interesting, as your club members determine the geologic history of the area in which they live. In many parts of our country it is possible to find dinosaur bones, fossils, and other evidences of prehistoric life. Museum trips are of value, too, for many exhibits will motivate the pupils to do work on their own. Collecting rocks, identifying them, and looking for fossils add to the interest. Photography should be incorporated with geology for permanent records, and for the fun of taking pictures. Picnics add to the gaiety of the field trips, and are a wonderful way to spend many pleasant afternoons socializing and health building.

CLUBS RELATED TO THE LANGUAGE ARTS

Literary

How do you make a literary club appealing? By advertising it as a great help when one gets to college, by specifying the books which will be read and choosing these books wisely (and with appeal for the children), and by the leader personally inviting the boys and girls he feels will benefit from it, enjoy it and be an asset to it—this club would be especially suitable for children who are attuned to literature.

By offering the pupils lists of books, allowing them to make choices, and then reading and discussing these books, the club can give the youngsters experiences they will not get otherwise. Such books as *For Whom the Bell Tolls, Caine Mutiny, Exodus, Catcher in the Rye, Moby Dick,* are all suitable beginnings. Short stories, too, may be considered—Edgar Allan Poe, A. Conan Doyle, Ernest Hemingway, or O'Henry, for example.

The leader's task is to help the characters come to life—help the youngsters to see them as real people, with real motives and emotions.

Poetry Club—with a Coffee House Approach

Both reading and writing poetry are parts of a Poetry Club. Here, too, the key is in finding relatively simple materials which will interest the youngsters. Then, as they become more sophisticated, they can be introduced to more complex poems. Mixing the modern poetry with the classical is good—for developing the children's taste and background.

Original poems written by the children may be read and enjoyed. Criticisms are unnecessary—they can spoil the atmosphere —and make the budding poets reticent about reading their works. They can actually destroy a child's talent. Encouragement rather than criticism is highly desirable. An informal atmosphere is essential, and stiffness and dignity should be avoided at all costs. A lounge rather than a classroom, would be preferable as a meeting place.

Drama

A drama group meeting to put on productions requires, in addition to the actors and actresses, directors, makeup people, stage hands, prompters, dressers and even ushers. (All of the children involved in the club should be given experience doing all of these jobs, as they do in summer stock theatre companies, to give them background.) If your club can be run by a leader who has had experience with theatre groups, it can be done as a "little theatre." Productions may be put on to raise money for the school, or for charitable purposes.

The plays which are attempted should be those which the children can understand and can master. They need not be too long— often the standard Broadway production is not suitable for such groups because of this. The choice of play should be made by the children, from a selection offered by the club leader. In this way both opinions are considered.

The drama club can be a source of great joy and satisfaction to the children—if they all get the chance to participate. And they all should!

Theatre Club

As contrasted to a drama club, a theatre club would study the theatre—would see plays, or read them, and then really study them. The members would discuss the structure of the play, the character development, the method the author uses to create suspense, the environment, the effect it has on the action of the play, and most important, the social and moral value of the play. They would study the crafts which are involved in play production, such as lighting, staging and even the changing of scenery. They might learn the methods for applying makeup and the making of costumes.

While a drama club prepares the youngsters to act, the theatre club prepares them for being an intelligent theatre-going audience, one which truly understands and appreciates the various aspects of stagecraft. Their study should range from the Greek Theatre, and the plays of yesteryear, to the Theatre of the Absurd, and the works of today.

Tape Recording Club

The tape recorder is a tool which may provide the basis for a fascinating club. Try tape recording such phenomena as the sounds of nature. We have a friend who did this in an open field at night (in Iowa); birds, crickets and animals, plus the sound of the wind made a most beautiful record. The listener is transported to this peaceful, natural spot, but because he hears without seeing, his imagination furnishes the background. The result is a highly poetic experience. We, ourselves, heard the tape, and were delighted with it. The tape recorder is a magic carpet with which the skilled operator can take us anywhere—to places of wonder and delight.

Try taping the sounds of the city or of traffic rushing along the highways. Perhaps you might enjoy hearing the sounds of the harbor on a foggy night. Tape a trip to a World's Fair, or to a state fair—and the experiences are preserved long after the fair has vanished. Children playing, a visit to a zoo, an evening at an amusement park, the excitement of the Fourth of July are all worthy of taping. Events of world-wide importance, taped from radio or television programs that are particularly meritorious or interesting, can be brought out years later and enjoyed. Events in school, too, such as special assemblies or graduation exercises, plays or debates, furnish excellent material for tape recording.

The Movie Club

The movie club is one which is sure to interest many children. Very often reduced rates are obtainable, for the tickets are bought in large numbers. The keynote, however, must be a decision that the movies selected will have moral and social worth. They must all be previewed by the leader.

An "Underground Newspaper"

We are acquainted with many young people anxious to establish their own newspapers, with their own views. What makes the situation interesting is that they are perfectly willing, in many cases, to do this within the framework of a club, and with a faculty advisor. These youngsters want to be guided, but also want to have their say. Their policies may be different from those of the school or national administration, but an agreement can and must be reached wherein they will go along with certain rules and regulations, such as the outlawing of language which is in bad taste.

Such a newspaper gives the children another opportunity to have their say, but with adult supervision, and this makes it emotionally as well as intellectually satisfying. With this procedure in mind, disorders may possibly be precluded. It is a channel for the youngsters' emotions, which might otherwise find an outlet in destructive and anti-social behavior.

CLUBS IN CONNECTION WITH SOCIAL STUDIES

Discussion Club

Related to the social studies department, we encourage the establishment of a *discussion* club. Many of our young people are very involved with the affairs of the day, and are very anxious for a place to discuss them. They are, in actuality, looking for a place to air their views, but will, if forced to, listen to the other side as well. It is possible to set up persons acting as the "Devil's Advocates" who will argue the other side of important issues, thus stimulating discussion. One-sidedness is to be avoided, however, because it becomes uninteresting, unchallenging and is intellectually narrowing.

Have the children suggest topics they wish to discuss, and give them time to prepare for the sessions. This will require doing research, because it is extremely important that they be well-informed, and not use half-truths or misconceptions. The strength of their discussions or debates will depend in large measure on their preparation.

Polling Political Opinion

During election years, and in the past five years, interest in current events has run very high. Polling by such as by Messrs. Gallup and Harris has become big business. Children interested in doing polling can effectively sample members of the school and community. In doing this, care should be taken to prepare questions which will be absolutely inoffensive, and which will not put words into people's mouths. As an added bonus, this is an interesting way in which to get the children to communicate with the older people.

Consumer's Club

We all belong to the family of consumers; and because, in the course of our lifetimes we all spend large sums of money, a club of this kind can have great value. Its work can include shopping for best buys, research using publications such as *Consumer's Reports,* and learning how to differentiate the good from the bad —in all areas, from furniture to cosmetics, from food to fortune telling.

Speakers, visits to factories, communications with local representatives of city, state and federal agencies such as the Better Business Bureaus, can make this club an exciting and stimulating club.

World Problems

The people of the world are faced with many problems which are present regardless of their economic or political state. Air pollution, for example, is to be found in all parts of the world. The skies over cities or towns are often filled with a mixture of gases which causes death and destruction. London, New York, Los Angeles, are all famous for their haze—and even Mexico City, 7,000 feet above sea level, lies beneath a blanket of smog.

Food production has not kept up with the population increases, and, if we continue as we have been, the famines which must come will kill off untold millions of people. We must find ways to solve this problem—and our time is limited.

These are but two of the very serious problems facing the entire world. What can a club do to help solve them? The children become aware of the situation, discuss it, and seek ways to take action. Writing letters is one. Investigating one's own area to find what is causing such a problem as pollution is another.

Speakers, visits, research, all contribute. Putting out reports, helping to educate the school and community to the dangers, writing letters to the newspapers, are all methods by which educated citizens can work to improve their community and the world.

Much is achieved by activities of this kind to make the child mindful of the needs of others. He is taken out of himself, and altruistic interests are awakened, making him a better citizen not only of our country, but of the world. The little boy who is busy raising money for the needy is far less likely to be anti-social—for his emotions are channeled toward constructive and philanthropic activities.

Foreign Language Clubs

We suggest clubs be offered in those languages which are not part of your normal curriculum. Chinese, Italian, Swahili and Hebrew are only some of the possibilities. In this area, it would be wisest to offer the actual choice to the children.

Obviously the leader of a foreign language club must be skilled in the language. He should lead the organization as a club, being very careful to avoid a classroom atmosphere. Informality, friendliness and conversation are the keynotes. Vocabulary lists of words, which the children request as they try to speak, and to convey their ideas, should be developed. In the beginning, books should be avoided, if at all possible.

Games, such as "Simon Sez" are amusing as well as excellent teaching tools for use in the club situation. Cartoons, skits, songs and stories all are preferable to formal lessons.

Stress the novelty of the language. Encourage the children to speak with their families—to teach them bits of the language they are learning. You may give parties, with decorations, refreshments, songs and dances, anecdotes and jokes, related to the language being studied.

African, Persian, Indian or Japanese Culture

Clubs which are devoted to these ancient cultures, to the lives of the people, their art and their contributions to the modern world may appeal to some children.

Connected with this should be trips to museums, speakers, slide shows, films, records and research. The club members may be involved in the art of the era, or the history, the music or the customs. The more fascinating the study is made, the more children will become involved. Enthusiasm is an absolute essential, for without it the program falls flat.

CLUBS ASSOCIATED WITH MATHEMATICS

The Stock Market

"The Bulls and the Bears" might be the name of a club which is interested in securities, and the workings of the stock market. Reading the quotations, following various issues, and visiting brokerage houses are activities for this club. If it is at all feasible, a visit to the New York Stock Exchange on Wall Street is surely in order. Speakers are often valuable resource persons, but the club leader must be careful that the young people are not pressured by them. Performance levels of stocks and "the market" in both good and bad years, should be included so that no child gets a false picture of the investment field.

You may include a study of a large corporation, so that the children fully comprehend the meaning of the words "shares in the company," and a visit to this company's offices might be arranged. Choosing a corporation with branches or plants in your community may heighten the interest, or your youngsters may decide they are more intrigued by some of the industrial giants.

Computers

Surely one of the most important tools of today, and even more so of tomorrow, the computer is the most significant advance in modern technology. For those so inclined, a club which visits computer installations, studies their workings, and even enables young people to build simple, working models, is very valuable. It stimulates the imagination of these gifted children, giving them excellent opportunities to become part of the fascinating world of tomorrow.

ART CLUBS

Within the art department there are a number of clubs which may be created. All can contribute to the child's development as a person, can give him a pleasurable activity for leisure hours, and can possibly supply him with a hobby or vocation for his entire lifetime.

Painting or Drawing, Fashion Design,
   Ceramics, Sculpture, Cartooning or Sketching

If you have a large number of children interested, set up separate clubs for beginners and for advanced students. In each be sure there is more to the club than merely a studio in which to work. However, the leader should give help *only* if he is asked for it—it is so easy to kill the children's interest. One of the authors has hanging on the wall of her living room a painting done by her daughter at the age of 10. She was thrilled that the child showed as much talent, and rushed her into an art "club" with a private teacher. That ended her career. After three sessions she never picked up a brush again! No amount of discussion could determine why.

If beginners are in the same group as children who are more proficient, they get discouraged and quit. Also these youngsters need instruction in where to start—how to get their work into progress. Since their needs are entirely different, if different clubs are established they are far better than one. If this is impossible, the leader should divide the group, and work with each half.

The youngsters' work should be kept on exhibit at all times. If there are boys and girls who are especially talented, the leader may arrange for them to have one-man shows in the school or in the community. We have found people in banks, libraries and stores are anxious and willing to set up such exhibitions. Theatre lobbies, airports and restaurants are possibilities, as well. There

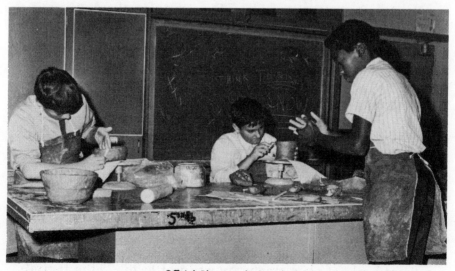

—Official Photograph, Board of Education, City of New York

YOUNGSTERS EXPLORING THE FIELD OF POTTERY-MAKING

should, however, be an art gallery in the school where the pupils' work is constantly exhibited. Trips to museums and galleries are of value—and add to the interest the club can give to the children.

Architecture and Interior Design

One of the least publicized hobby fields, an interest in architecture accompanied by the construction of models, can be a basis for a wonderful club, and often leads to a fine vocation for some of the youngsters. In different parts of our country, many intriguing new buildings are rising, and these can be the cornerstone for the leader to build upon. Speakers, visits, and films will add interest, and building scale models may be a source of satisfaction for many youngsters.

If desired, interior design may be added to the topic, for here, too, there are so many new ideas and concepts in evidence today. We cite the use of plastics, of lights, of inflatable furniture to name but a few—this is the "mod world" at its most practical. Many department stores, for example, have exhibits of current trends in interior design, and after visiting these, the boys and girls can adapt their own ideas. Encourage creativity—there is a huge field for it when the young people enter the world of work. And as nothing else can, creativity defeats the boredom that so often blights the daily job.

Photography and Movie Making

Both aspects of the cameraman's art may be included in your club offering. In addition to practicing these arts, the boys and girls should get experience in appreciating them. Taking pictures, developing them, printing, enlarging and composing will be enjoyed by the children. Writing scripts for movies and editing and cutting them are experiences which a film-making club may give to its members.

Attending photography exhibits, and studying the various magnificant books of photographs are well worthwhile. Film festivals, reviewing the history of film making, and considering the cinematographer's objectives, add to the thrill of making a movie, for the youngsters can learn from the masters.

Music

Guitar, rock and roll, folk singing, quartets—music clubs can offer a great variety which will appeal to many of the children. Guitar clubs are popular, with the recorder or other instruments possibilities, as well. Folk singing, singing groups, rock 'n roll bands, barbershop quartets will attract large numbers of members. We feel that all clubs should stress participation, rather than listening to recorded music. "Battles of the Bands" between rock groups are exciting—albeit noisy to the adult ear.

Suggest that each music club make tapes to submit for auditions. This makes practice and perfecting the sound essential. The pupils in the school can enjoy hearing the groups, too, and performances should be planned with this in mind.

Music Appreciation

We feel our children should be introduced to "good music" through excellent recordings, so that the youngsters who are already attuned to this will get the opportunities to hear them. Perhaps it will awaken a dormant musical ear in children who appear insensitive to this type of music. And incidentally, let us remember the famous words, "Music has charms to soothe."

A Record Club

We suggest a club based on the appreciation of records or tapes of all kinds—musical, poetic, excerpts from great plays or operas, or any other type of recording. The children should be encouraged to bring in records or tapes, especially those of their own making. Instruction can be given in the recording techniques, and you may have an exchange of records or ideas. A club of this sort might be the nucleus for a record lending library.

HOME ECONOMICS CLUBS

Sewing

Within the area of home economics are many areas which lend themselves to club activities. We recall being told by a group of girls that they "desperately" wanted a sewing club. What was odd was the time of the year—it was February. They insisted and persisted. Finally the reason came out—they were most anxious to make their own Easter outfits.

Sewing and some simple designing can be handled in one club. Encourage the girls to use originality in their work, by their use of color, for example. They can vary patterns, too, to design their own dresses. The club leader has an opportunity to have one girl help another, in this club situation, thus fostering friendship as well as teaching sewing. Creating accessories should be included, as well as clothing. Here, too, is an area wherein creativity can be developed.

Cooking

Cooking is fun—especially when boys as well as girls are invited to join the club. As evidenced by the fact that most of the best chefs are men, the young gentlemen should be encouraged to enjoy the culinary art—from the performance as well as the consumer angle.

Your members may decide they wish to specialize in foreign cookery, or in baking, in sauces or in candies. Take a vote, and follow their leads.

Be sure to have this club "cater" some of the school parties, and "show off" their products. Cakes, candy and cookies are products which can be used for fund-raising, and provide the club members with opportunities to serve the school.

CLUBS UNRELATED TO ACADEMIC SUBJECTS

The Game Club

A place to play dominoes or casino, Monopoly or Scrabble, the game room is the spot, also, for socializing with one's friends. None of the pursuits listed are really serious ones, but they serve to bring children together for fun and for companionship. The tasks of the leader are to introduce youngsters to one another, and to make everyone feel comfortable. He must also be sure that the situation does not get over-heated at any point. The boys and girls should be permitted to bring in games of their own, and the room should be open to everyone who wishes to use it. Rooms of this type are popular in colleges, where they serve as the social hall and the meeting place.

The room chosen for this should be a large one—the cafeteria of the school is often excellent. This is the place which will serve as almost a second home to some of the children. As well as the leader, there should be representatives of the Student Government present to supervise, depending on the number of children who attend. You will find this will be greatest in the winter time, and less as the spring and summer approach. This room will probably be very well attended at the beginning of the school year—too well, in fact, but this often changes as the term progresses.

By making the atmosphere warm and inviting, a really deep need may be fulfilled for those children whose homes are, for one reason or another, not particularly pleasant places. It is also an excellent place for those children, who have few friends in the immediate vicinity of their homes, and who seek companionship. This is true in affluent suburbs, probably more often than in other areas.

Your Student Government may vote to serve pretzels and hot chocolate, or Coca-Cola in this room. If so, be sure there is a clean-up squad, as well, and that the project is self-supporting. Informality, and a spirit of gaiety should prevail. This often reflects the personality of the person in charge, and it, therefore, is so important to find the right individual for this situation.

Chess and Checkers

Allied to the game room, but, of necessity separated from it, you may have a chess and checkers club. The atmosphere must be different from the game room, however, for both games require concentration and a relatively quiet atmosphere. Tournaments and contests add to the excitement, and should be arranged. This is easily done by the Student Government.

It is an excellent idea to offer instruction in both of these games, for both are pursuits which can be of great value to the boys and girls as they mature. Try to interest the young ladies as well as the young gentlemen.

You may invite guest speakers to discuss the games, possibly to give instructions, and even to compete with some of the students. Teachers and parents, too, may be invited to play in competitions. The school might even offer a trophy to the champion, and he might enter competitions outside of the school.

School Service

One of the most valuable clubs, and one which can be extremely gratifying—is a school service club. Children enjoy doing service— from ushering at school functions and working on monitorial squads, to serving coffee at Parent-Teacher Association meetings.

Clean-up campaigns, beautification programs, clothing collections, fund-raising operations and charitable endeavors are all possibilities.

This club will appeal to a very special type of child—and give him an outlet for his philanthropic impulses. Surely the school should foster such impulses—for the essential work which is performed by such individuals, not only in school, but throughout their lives.

Be sure that trips are planned—to the local chapter of the American Red Cross, for example, or to a hospital in your area.

However, rewarding expeditions should be included, as well, particularly if the boys and girls have worked hard.

COLLECTING

The joys of collecting are many and varied—and, as hobbies almost unsurpassed. The collector often feels he is achieving success, is using his time in what he considers to be a worthwhile manner, and is able to pursue his interest to the extent he wishes. By forming clubs for collectors, we invite them to share their enthusiasms, and in some cases our boys and girls are introduced to activities which may subsequently become vocations.

In our clubs, we must stress the worthiness of the item collected *in terms of its interest value, rather than its cash value,* in terms of what may be learned from it, and in terms of the joy and satisfaction it brings to its owner—rather than its price in the market place.

Stamps

More people probably collect stamps than any other item. By grouping interested youngsters, we give them opportunities to trade and to admire. We should, however, include sessions on the care of stamps, on how to obtain them, and on their history or stories. The excitement of finding very valuable stamps should be considered. Speakers may be invited to share their knowledge with the boys and girls. We vividly recall Captain Tim Healy, a radio personality of many years ago, whose program was based on stories behind stamps. New, unusual, fascinating issues make the most exciting items to collect.

Coins

Coin collecting can have many different aspects: Coins from foreign lands, or coins from our own; pennies minted in different years (and sometimes worth unbelievable sums of money because of their rarity), or half dollars. In this area, too, there are many opportunities for the individual to follow his own interests.

Nature Studies

Seashells, rocks, dried flowers, seeds or leaves are but a few of the many possibilities collections of nature's gifts offer. Any of these offer a great deal because the collector becomes interested in that aspect of natural science. These hobbies are good, too, because they take the collector out into the fresh air and sunshine of the seashore, or the fields and forests, and they open his eyes to the wonderful world around him.

Picture postcards, matchbook covers, menus, magazines, dolls costumed in the native dress of foreign nations, posters, books, paper weights, photographs—all are possible items for club membership. It may be desirable to form a collectors' club, and encourage anyone collecting anything to belong. In this way, children will learn from one another, and share their interests and enthusiasms.

FINDING YOUR VOCATION CLUB

What could be a more important issue to young people than finding their vocations? For many of them, this is an issue they are reluctant to face, but, in the context of a club, it is possible to get a great deal of information to them. This club should be based entirely on the needs of the individual members. These should be determined, and then speakers invited, interviews set up, and many, many visits arranged. Future aviators, models, lawyers, technicians, and the myriad of occupations under consideration should become part of the club's agenda. Indeed, this list should be as long, and as varied, as there are children interested.

Stenography and Typing

For those children who would like to study these skills, a club situation is often very desirable. A system of speedwriting may be given relatively quickly—and is invaluable for high school and college students. Typing may be learned from books and phonograph records.

Both skills will benefit the college bound student—and often he is not able to fit these subjects into his regular school program. The club, thereby, can solve a need. But, to make it seem more like a club, activities are needed such as contests, tournaments and picture drawing with the typewriters.

You may wish to try programmed learning for this club. These are subjects which can be handled in this manner, and which might prove to be an interesting experiment.

Choosing Your College

Differing from finding-your-vocation, this club devotes its energies to learning about schools and colleges—their requirements, their specialties and their preferences. Speakers from the colleges can be invited, and visits to them, plus discussion by students and counselors would make up the program—an obviously worthwhile one—from which even junior high school, as well as high school students, could benefit.

PSYCHOLOGY

Of the subjects children are often most interested in, psychology ranks as one of the most attractive. The study of the mind, and of human behavior can be the basis for a number of clubs which will intrigue them.

Basic, normal psychology—why people act as they do—is the starting point for one. The laws of learning, the conscious and the subconscious mind—the variety of topics is endless, as is the amount of material on film. For example, even though it is theatrical, a child would love to see and then discuss "The Three Faces of Eve."

Family Living and Sex Education

Parental permission is a necessity for such a club. Here, stress the practical approach—the discussion of problems—the children should be encouraged to bring these up. It may be more practical for the leader to initiate them—but once the club has started to roll, the boys and girls will begin to discuss things which are bothering them, and ask for specific information they want. Often an informal situation such as this enables young people to really speak out, to talk about problems which are troubling them. And very often they discover their peers have similar problems. A club of this sort can help the boys and girls set standards for themselves, or can aid them in understanding those which their parents have established. Curfews, for example, when discussed by a group, invariably are better accepted. When Jane discovers that Bill has to be home at 10:00, her deadline doesn't seem so terrible. The universality of the nature of the problems makes this club of great value. We believe that children with problems will be attracted to this club, in the same manner that they usually find classmates with similar problems with whom to be friends.

ESP and Psychic Phenomena

This club offers a fascinating study to the children. No mere recitations of ghost stories, although these should certainly be included, this club should do actual experiments in extra-sensory perception. There are many references available, suggesting possible experiments with playing cards and specially made materials. The Ouija Board, fortune telling by cards or tea leaves, even crystal ball gazing, all heighten interest. The leader of this club however, must be someone who feels that extra-sensory perception does exist. If he is negative in this regard, very few experiments will work. But this club can be, with the proper leadership, a really stimulating experience.

ATHLETICS

Tennis, Golf, Bowling, Handball and Physical Fitness

The world of sports offers a great variety from which to choose. However, we would like to see first preference given to those activities which will carry over into the pupil's life after he leaves school. These include tennis, golf, bowling, handball and, most important, a program of physical fitness. Each of these activities can be enjoyed by the individual at his leisure. Each, however, is far more pleasant if one has developed skill at it—and a club program can help to foster this. One important aspect is that the club offer *instruction* in the sport, for without it, the children will falter, and their achievement and satisfaction will be limited. This is not to say that the leader must be a professional. However, he should be someone who knows how to play the game, and feels enthusiastic about it. Competitions, tournaments, and teams add to the excitement.

It is possible to combine several of these sports. Tennis, bowling and golf might be combined, or even any two of the three. You might arrange any combination of these sports, to suit the child. Physical fitness is a particularly important one, for it can lead to a lifetime pursuit of a goal which pays huge dividends in terms of good health.

Please note: These sports and the ones which follow should not be limited to boys. Girls need them as much, if not more so, for they tend, for the most part, to be less athletically inclined.

Baseball, Basketball, Volleyball, Football

These are essentially team sports, but we feel that, if there is a demand, every boy or girl should be able to take part in them, regardless of the skill he or she has achieved. Many schools have teams, but no other opportunity is provided. By having a club, and here, too, it is essental that instruction be given, every child can play. The clubs will supply other needs. They can serve as "farm teams" supplying talent for the school team. The farm teams can play against the school, or varsity team, giving the latter practice. (This should be done, even if the farm team is much weaker. Give them points, if necessary, to make the contest more feasible.)

Roller and Ice Skating, Skiing and Sledding

If your area offers facilities, these winter sports are all very valuable because they offer the children more skills which they will turn to when adults, and, in this era, participating gives the children salutary outlets for their energies. As with many other activities, doing them with a group is more fun than alone—and groups of enthusiasts will develop to carry the club along. Here, too, combinations of activities are practical, for weather conditions have a great influence on the availability of opportunity.

Swimming, Water Skiing, Scuba Diving and Sailing

Special facilities are, of course, necessary, for clubs of this nature. However, they are often available at relatively low fees—if the use of the facilities of other agencies is considered. Canvas your area, contact such agencies, and determine whether or not a program may be run. Usually there are certain "off days," when this is possible. Commercial organizations, too, should be approached for they are often willing and anxious to cooperate—at less than their usual fee scales.

Dancing—Social, Ballroom, Modern, Interpretive or Ballet

Without question, social dancing is one of the social skills children need. Many girls catch on very quickly, and require only a little instruction, but boys require more, and many times are reluctant to learn. They may be embarrassed or shy, but whatever the reason, at so many dances they line the walls—watching instead of participating.

Every school needs a club which offers instruction in the *latest dances*. The best instructors available for this are the youngsters in the school—usually the girls. A skillful leader brings them together, sets up conditions which minimize the embarrassment, and makes the members feel welcome.

Don't have members of another generation, unless they are professional dancers, well-versed in the latest "crazes" teach. One of the authors, at a school dance, watched several couples dancing, and said to them, "That's an adorable dance. What do you call it?" The reply, "Cha,cha," amazed her. She commented to herself, "That's not the way we do it." Indeed, there wasn't a bit of resemblance.

Other types of dancing may be offered—if there is a demand for them. So-called "ballroom dancing," with the foxtrot, rhumba and even the lindy, is one. Ballet, modern or interpretive dancing is another, which may be considered, if skilled teachers are available. The latter is excellent for musical productions for assembly programs or special occasions.

CLUBS TO DEVELOP A SENSE OF ACHIEVEMENT

Industrial Arts—Carpentry, Graphic Arts, Ceramics or Arts and Crafts

Clubs such as these are all very worthwhile, for they enable the children to develop feelings of achievement and success. Surely the projects selected should be those previously considered by the club leader, insuring the possible completion of most of them. The youngsters should also get the experiences of handling different tools and a variety of media. All of these clubs should be open to members of both sexes. Indeed, we believe girls should be urged to join, for if they have talents in these directions, the regular school curriculum does not bring them out.

Many schools have the necessary facilities for all of these clubs. The items created should be of two varieties—some which the children may make and then take home, and some produced for the school to sell. The latter must, of necessity, be of good quality. Their sale will bring in funds, which may, in turn, be used to purchase more materials.

In each of these areas, the broader the scope of the program, the more pleasure and value it will bring to the children. However, it must be stressed—this is a club, not a classroom, with different objectives and different conditions.

Trips should be injected, too, for variety and for pleasure. If there is a local theatre, might not the carpentry club enjoy seeing how the stage sets are made? The graphic art group could visit a local newspaper or print shop. Seeing a skilled watchmaker work is always fascinating, and other craftsmen, too, are worth contacting and visiting.

—Courtesy of Colonial Williamsburg, Virginia

COLONIAL WILLIAMSBURG, VIRGINIA

High school students watch a costumed craftsman fashion a peg by driving the wood through a pegging dolly. Pegs were used more often than nails in the 18th Century in furniture-making, flooring and roofing, and peg-making is one of some thirty colonial crafts demonstrated for visitors to Colonial Williamsburg. School visits can add a new dimension to classroom teaching of history, social studies, and decorative arts.

A gift shop in the school, selling inexpensive gifts, may be a real service to the children, and can be operated by the clubs, jointly. Give it a catchy name—"Clever Creations" would be far preferable to "Gift Shoppe."

Manual activities are very satisfying—and can become important aspects of the children's lives, sometimes leading to vocations, or lifetimes hobbies. For these reasons, such clubs should be fostered.

Babysitting Training and Service Club

Here is a club which not only gives valuable information to the children, but offers a service to the community. Be sure a certificate is given to the pupils who belong to the club, and have been trained, stating they have gotten this training. Their names should be published, and they may then join the staff to serve the public—and incidentally to help PTA meetings and other school functions.

Vacation Club and Travel

A vacation and travel club should discuss places to visit, and things to do—first in the immediate area, then farther afield.

—Photo Credit, U. S. Dept. of the Interior,
National Park Service, Edison National Historic Site

EDISON NATIONAL HISTORIC SITE

Children on tour at Edison National Historic Site view Thomas A. Edison's open desk.

Camping, hunting, sailing, fishing, mountain climbing may all be discussed. Slides and movies may be used to excellent advantage. Our National Parks are worth full study. Then the club can go on to thinking about trailers, or foreign travel, jets or jalopies.

Clubs with Pets

Obedience school and training for dogs is a service which a club may offer to the school population and to the community. It gives children a chance to work with their pets, and to learn to control them—so that the youngsters will assume this responsibility. *Gentleness, at all times, must be the keynote!*

A tropical fish club is another possibility, and one which may do service to the school by keeping a fish tank well stocked and clean and on display. It is necessary to have knowledgeable people —either as the leader or members—for a financial outlay is necessary. It is often possible to find people willing to donate equipment—tanks, filters, etc.

Pen Pals

A pen pal club, with the sharing of experiences, may bring to the boys and girls a very varied group of ideas. By choosing pen pals from many different far-away lands, and by sharing letters, the children can benefit from one another's contacts. This program can be made exciting by taking photographs, sending them to the pen pals, and hoping for reciprocation. If the boys and girls agree, these pictures may be placed on a bulletin board, with a short biography of the writer.

This type of program spreads world-wide good will. The people to people approach is one which is so necessary in the world today.

THE CLUB PROGRAM SUMMARIZED

We have listed many types of clubs separately which may readily be combined. For example, collecting stamps and coins; drawing and painting; baseball, football and volleyball; golf, bowling and tennis.

An extensive club program has a great deal to offer for it affords the children the opportunity to broaden their horizons and to pursue their interests. It supplies places for socializing as well as for learning, for fun as well as for experiences. But no one can force a child to join a club and really partake of its program. He must have the opportunity to choose his area—and it is with this in mind that we have suggested this inclusive listing of possible club activities. Every one of them, we are sure, has value—and it will, if properly functioning, bring knowledge and pleasure to its members and to its leader.

Encourage your children to "do their thing," to join a club of their liking, where they can meet new and interesting friends, with whom they will find much in common. A thinker once said, "We recognize friends—we do not make them." A club is the place where unknown friends are brought together through common interest and their recognition made easy.

You will want, therefore, to make your club program a success. We will discuss some of the aspects which affect the program, with specific information in regard to strengthening it.

The Club Leader

A club is not a classroom—if it is to be successful, the leader must go out of his way to emphasize this. We watched a club go from 45 members (too many, but all of the children had evidenced interest) to 14 (who remained because they felt sorry that everyone else was dropping out). The leader of the club, a young teacher, lectured at every meeting—and even required the children to take notes!

1) The leader should understand that he is not the authority figure in this situation. Often this is difficult to experience—particularly for an inexperienced teacher, who is struggling for control! However, this requires a change of role which is not only possible but also necessary and will additionally benefit the teacher, as well.

2) At the very first or second meeting elections are held, and the subsequent management of meetings turned over to the group. If there are youngsters who do not cooperate with their elected

officials, the leader takes them aside and speaks to them privately. Since clubs are not classrooms, membership should be considered a privilege, and treated as such. Do not force any child to remain. If he (or she) is not interested, it is pointless to keep him—and he can spoil the spirit of the club for the interested members. Moreover, the minute anything becomes a privilege, it takes on a completely different aspect.

We can illustrate this best by an anecdote from the classroom. A teacher-friend of ours tells her children, "You cannot read aloud if you do not listen to the other children. If you would like to read, you must be courteous. I'm sure every one of you is courteous, and we would like to hear you." It really works.

3) *The leader should become an expert.* To become really good at his task, he should be involved in the club, and should learn as much about the field as possible. By reading newspapers and magazines he can keep up with new ideas and new developments These should be brought to the attention of the members and, i necessary, duplicated and distributed—but without telling th children they must read them. Books are, of course, an excellen. source of information, but they should be recommended, not assigned, quoted but not force-fed. We are most anxious to get the children intrigued, and interested—but not coerced.

4) *Summit meetings.*—Club leaders within the school should get together from time to time to pool their resources, and to trade ideas. Often, if the "doldrums" have set in, in a particular club, the suggestions of other leaders can prove very helpful. Joint meetings of clubs, joint parties, and trips are all possibilities, and renewed enthusiasms are kindled.

Start with a Bang!

After elections have the children suggest activities they would like to do as part of the club program. Have the president preside, and the secretary take notes. There may be a profusion of suggestions, or very few. The leader, must be prepared with a list, so that if the children's imaginations lag, their thinking is initiated.

Basically, the list should include the following:

1) Several trips of interest. (We feel children love trips and so

we believe they are excellent devices. They add excitement, motivate—and are almost always worthwhile.)

2) *Something for nothing*—Everyone, no matter how affluent, loves to receive something for nothing. You may get such materials by sending away for them, by using school funds to purchase, or by asking for contributions from people you know. Stamps for example, are available in bulk—and usually relatively inexpensively. Children love sorting them out, and trading. Perhaps you know of a collector with a large number of "doubles" who will contribute them. But your children will be extremely happy to get something for nothing.

This should not be done too frequently, for, if it is, it loses its thrill—and, more serious, the children will expect such gifts.

3) Invite speakers—so that the members of the club do learn, do get information they didn't have before. Try, however, for vital, alive people. This is important. Remember: A speaker may be a teacher from your own school, or another, who is interested; a parent, a community member, or person well-known in the field. Ask the children if there is anyone they would like to invite, and, by all means, do so.

4) Every club should have some portion of its time devoted to serving others. For some this is simpler, for others a bit more complicated. The cooking club can prepare cookies or candy for donations to a hospital, for example. But each club should have some philanthropic aspect as one of its objectives. This is extremely important as part of the development of the children for it awakens a social conscience. By presenting this as a way of enriching both the donor and the recipient and by showing the children this is a way they can demonstrate their maturity, their beneficence, they can be persuaded to cooperate beautifully. Encourage them to make their own decisions—to work out their own projects.

5) Every club should plan one party. It may be in school or at the home of one of the members. (A parental invitation is absolutely a necessity.) It may be a picnic or a trip, a boat ride or a masquerade, but a party is a must. It should be planned for at the very beginning of the year. The children should be told to think about it, so they have time to decide on something they will enjoy.

A ballgame, a television broadcast, a show or a movie may be substituted—but try for a gala event.

6) Plan a calendar, but stress the fact that it should be flexible, and easily changed. Try to have some feature for each meeting, something for the children to look forward to.

You may invite outsiders to meetings; other clubs may be asked to hold meetings with you; or parents may be requested to come to specific meetings.

Children can give presentations, but only if they would like to do so. Let's face it, there are children who love to be "on stage"—and others who do not. Try to get volunteers—children who need this sort of attention—and can benefit from it.

7) Find a place in which the materials and equipment needed can be stored. Nothing can cause people to lose interest more quickly than having to hunt for their things each time the club meets.

8) If a club can benefit from meeting in places other than in the school, try to set these up. A tennis club, for example, might benefit by playing on clay courts, on composition or all-weather, and even, for experience, on the grass courts (from which the name "lawn tennis" is derived).

9) *Expand the children's interests.* Bring in related fields—so that the club experience is broadening. In the current music appreciation—which would surely concern itself with "rock," bring in the antecedents—the jazz, blues, and African music which preceded it. You might try, deftly, to introduce the masters—Bach, for example, Beethoven, or Shubert.

10) *Present tokens at the end of the year for attendance.* Because clubs are not part of the curriculum, and because attendance must not be made mandatory, there should be some recognition given for good attendance. We suggest charms or tie tacks with a suitable emblem. These may even be sold at cost to those boys and girls desirous of purchasing them—who have met the attendance requirements. Certificates are another possibility, but these should be handsome, printed, almost diploma like in style.

11) Allow the children freedom to sit where they please, and to move around. Again, we stress, this is not a classroom situation. Informality should be the keynote, and sociability encouraged.

If school rules permit, refreshments may be served—simple ones such as Coke or ice cream, cookies or fruit are adequate.

12) Each club should put out a newssheet or a newspaper. If there are a number of clubs in the school, a newssheet might be preferable—for these can then be combined to form a paper.

Each child's name should be mentioned in the club report. This is extremely important for the self-images of the children— and to describe to the parents and the community the activities which are going on in the club program.

13) Photographing the club meetings and activities, and exhibiting the photographs is another form of excellent public relations. Club bulletin boards filled with pictures should line the hallways of the school, and particularly the front lobby. It is possible that the photography club members may be capable of taking the pictures.

14) Each year, an assembly program should be devoted to a discussion of the work and achievements of the various clubs. This should be given by the members rather than the leaders, and invitations should be extended for the following year.

CONCLUSION

To summarize, the following should be remembered:

1. Clubs should be chosen to fit the children's needs. Don't allow them to exceed 20 pupils, if possible. Clubs do not have to meet once a week. Every two weeks is a possibility, too.

2. If necessary, parents or members of the community may serve as leaders. They should, however, be given instructions in running the club.

3. Choose a clever, attractive name for the club. There is much in a name (to disagree with friend, Will).

4. Every club should have objectives, decided upon by the children and the leader.

5. *No club should be run like a class—never, under any circumstances!*

6. Make meetings exciting. Have things happening which the children will enjoy.

7. Schedule at least one trip during each year.

8. Plan a school-wide exposition for parents, community, and for students. Include exhibits of every club. You may wish to call it, "Expo 70 at Central High."

9. At the end of the year have the children evaluate each club.

10. A club may easily become a nucleus for the development of friendships—and so loneliness and its disastrous side effects are defeated. Intellectual interests are born, fomented, nurtured and eagerly shared. None of us ever has too many friends. It is hoped that the leader will do everything to foster sociability and a warm feeling among the members.

Athletic Teams   **5**
and Cheerleaders

Has your school periods of "doldrums"? Do you find that there is little school spirit? Are your pupils apathetic? We believe that, if your answers are in the affirmative, we have a possible remedy—in a program involving many athletic teams and cheerleaders.

Because sports competitions are of interest to the young, because boys and girls become involved in and enthused about them, and because sports can serve as the media by which the needs of many children are fulfilled, we suggest the establishment of an extensive competitive sports program.

THE NEED FOR TEAMS AND CHEERLEADERS

One hundred years ago, Princeton and Rutgers played the first intercollegiate football game. Since then the game has spread far and wide, to almost every high school and college in our land.

Why should these high school and collegiate competitive sports be so popular? By competitive sports, we refer to baseball, basketball, track and football. Of course other types of teams are possibilities as well—tennis, bowling, swimming and sailing are but a few. As we discuss the need for teams, we include girls teams and cheerleaders as well, for we believe girls, as well as boys, should be involved in this type of activity. As individuals they need them equally as much, and will benefit from them as surely as the young men will. And what specific benefits will be derived by the school?

1) They help to instill school spirit, and to improve the morale

of the students. Young people, and many adults, too, love these team games—they enjoy playing them or observing them. Their appeal is tremendous—and concurrent with this appeal are inculcated feelings of belonging. The person is part of the game which he enjoys—and of the school—and of the entire scene. It is almost as if one is saying, "Central has a good football team. Central is my school. Yea, team!" The color and the pleasure associated with the game are transferred to the school.

2) Students have an outlet for their emotions as they cheer their teams to victory—or even as they bemoan defeat. The young people have an interest on which to focus their attention. They have games and a season to look forward to, and they have heroes of their own to worship. Who is a bigger man on campus than the football hero? Who has more prestige than an all-American?

3) The team gives the non-academic student an opportunity to shine—to be a big fish in the school pond. The boy who may have trouble passing math may be well able to pass that football. In the high school age group playing on the team is often the deciding factor for youngsters considering dropping out of school. Our so-called non-academic students are often boys and girls who have never known success in school—and who attain it for the first time through athletic accomplishment.

In every one of the three items mentioned above, the cheerleaders are as important as the teams, and should be thought of in conjunction with them.

The size of the school population, the availability of suitable coaches, the amount of financing possible and the feelings of the local school board will determine the number of teams a school may have. There may be baseball, basketball, football, track teams —and these may be divided into varsity, junior varsity or even grade teams. These are decisions for the school administration to make, based on the factors listed above.

THE COACH

In discussing teams we must stress the importance of the coach of the team. It is he who sparks the team, who instructs it, and who corrects its errors. We are all familiar with the names of famous college coaches—men who have remained renowned through the years. This fame is commensurate with their deeds, for the coach must be teacher, parent and friend to each child on the team. He must select his team from among all of the applicants, and must be able to recognize potential as well as achievement. It is his task to make the team function together—and to develop the spirit of cooperation and teamwork which must pervade the entire group.

It is imperative that the coach be an outgoing person who feels a genuine affection for young people. If he does, he will be able to work with them and bring out the best they have to offer. If he is unpleasant or arbitrary, or if he is dogmatic or unfair, his efficacy will diminish considerably. To put it simply, the young people must want to please him. He must also be able to convey his ideas to them clearly and succinctly, he must be extremely knowledgeable in regard to his field, and he must have the ability to convey such knowledge.

There are a number of ways in which team members may be selected. They may be recommended by health education teachers, or they may be volunteers. Regardless, each child who so desires should be given a chance to try out for the team of his choice, provided, of course, his health record does not prohibit his participation in this sport. Final selection must be by the coach, who should have the power to make all necessary decisions. It is he who assigns positions, trains and guides the players. He must be aware, too, of the need to plan for a continuing team—so that he will have players from year to year—and will train his team with this in mind.

We would hope the coach will give opportunities to the child who needs to develop, as well as to the one who has already done much work to perfect himself. Most assuredly, the coach has much responsibility to shoulder and his tasks are demanding ones.

TEAMWORK

Above everything else, teamwork should be stressed, for this is training for life as well as for athletics. The student who has learned to work for the good of the team, rather than for his own glory, has learned one of life's most important lessons. This type of learning is not come by easily, for it may be difficult for the youngster to function in this way. He may understand the basic idea, but being able to translate it into action is another thing. The best interests of the team must come before those of any one member. No one can see himself as a star, although often stars do emerge. But the work, the sheer effort of attaining a common goal must be brought out again and again. It may be necessary for the coach to work with individuals who cannot play in this manner, to make them understand the objective of teamwork. He may have to spend hours at this task, alone.

The team must develop a collective "mind"—by discussion, by establishment of principles, by reviewing procedures again and again, and by repeating and reiterating the concept that the welfare of each individual must be subordinated to the welfare of the team. They must take the coach's words as if they were law. This is not the time for individual initiative, but for collective and cooperative action. Games are won by teams, not by individuals. The part each member plays must be given importance if the team is to flourish, but he must be aware he is one part of many who make up the entire team.

To assist the coach with this, student managers and leaders may be used. Each team should have a student captain who motivates the team, sparks the games and who works almost as a liaison between the coach and the team. He is the boy who, very often, when he becomes a working adult, becomes a coach. He should have many of the same characteristics as the coach—the most important being an ability to work with the people on the team. It is strongly suggested that he be elected by his teammates, because, theoretically, they will then be more inclined to cooperate with him.

A student business manager and business staff is also usually chosen. Generally these are boys who are not of team caliber and who, by this association, link themselves with the team. This serves as an outlet for students who are interested, and can contribute in this way to the team's success. The student business manager may be placed in charge of ticket sales, advertising and the promotion of the team.

The cheerleading squad, we have found, is usually extremely motivated. Indeed, we have never seen any activity more self-directed and more self-executed. The girls of our squad, one year, made their own beautiful uniforms over the summer, and practiced, as well, during the eights weeks of vacation. Cheerleading carries a good deal of status, and since the cheerleaders see more of the members of the team, socially, than other girls, it is a most fought-for membership. We have had excellent cheerleaders taught by the girls themselves, and have seen more new cheers developed, and more precision attained, than we ever thought possible.

Cheerleaders should elect a student captain to assist the coach— or as she is usually called, the faculty advisor. She should be a person similar in personality to a coach—one who understands young girls. (Just being young herself does not insure this.) She should be able to lead the cheerleaders until student leaders are developed.

ESTABLISHING RULES

Rules must be set up for every team—and these must then be followed *to the letter*. This is an essential part of training boys and girls for college athletics (and incidentally for self-discipline). It also helps to develop championship teams. Your coach may either set up the rules, or work with the team to establish them. (The latter procedure is preferable, but for expediency, it may not be possible.)

How large should a team be? This depends on a number of factors. First, how large is the school, and how many teams are there. If there is a varsity, a junior varsity and a team of students from each grade, then each team need not be as large as if there were only a varsity and a junior varsity. We believe as many children as possible should be able to participate, for the teams are to serve the children as well as to bring glory to the school. Equally important, all interested students should be encouraged to join, or at least to try out for the teams of their choice.

Certain minimum standards of behavior and scholarship should be made mandatory for all team members and cheerleaders. The team captains should be responsible for making the team members aware of these standards, and should assist in enforcing them. Deviations from them should be punished, the penalty agreed upon long before the transgression. If a boy fails a subject, the penalty will have been established previously and the boy, himself, aware of it. Team membership often motivates boys to work harder in school than they ever worked before. We have all heard of some football players who manage to get by—with a little bit of help from their friends. If standards are not maintained, the team loses its beneficial aspect in so far as the students are concerned.

FUND RAISING

In many communities funds are available for athletic teams, but in others they are not. To raise funds, we suggest you use any or all of the following:

1. Charging for admission to games.
2. Appealing to the Parent-Teacher Association for partial, if not full, support.
3. Appealing to business people in the community for sponsorship.
4. Holding an annual dinner-dance for alumni parents and students with a printed program (for advertisements). Tickets may be priced so that sufficient funds are brought in to cover expenses for the year.
5. Fund raising within the school through a store run by the student government, where school supplies and school items are sold.
   Dances, cake sales, fairs are other ways to raise money.
6. *Candy sales.* There are a number of candy manufacturing companies which package candy to be resold by organizations, for the express purpose of raising money. Success with this kind of activity may be phenomenal, and thousands of dollars may be raised. Incidentally, the child who has a talent for

salesmanship will benefit greatly from this activity. We knew a boy who was not academically, nor sports oriented—but given a number of boxes of candy to sell, he surprised everyone by the prodigious number of his sales, and so revealed a tremendous business acumen we never suspected he had. The child had found himself. He was a born salesman.

7. Raffles, if permitted by law in your state, are excellent devices, for they are enjoyed by grown-ups and children as well as raising money.
   Bazaars and carnivals, too, are useful.

8. *Trips*—with a profit motive. If you wish, children may be taken on long trips, and charged for the trip with a contribution added on—for the school fund. For example, a group might be conducted to Washington, D.C. with this in mind.

9. *Suppers*—food cooked and contributed by the parents, or possibly the students, may be sold—and the profits used for support of the teams. Be sure the food is wholesome and attractive before embarking on this venture. Desserts can be served for this purpose in the school cafeteria.

10. Theatre parties are excellent in those communities fortunate enough to have legitimate theatres, or located closely enough to be reached by busses. The latter may be hired for an evening, and a package deal involving theatre and dinner offered either to parents, students, or both. This type of activity, in addition to raising funds, is often a very welcome addition to the social life of the community and awakens and fosters a love of the theatre.

INTER- AND INTRA-SCHOOL COMPETITION

Teams imply competition, and this may be created in many ways. If there are a number of schools, with boys and girls of similar ages, in your area, inter-school games should be established, and by holding them year after year, traditions will grow. "Midtown High always beats South High," the students may say, but they are interested, nevertheless. This activity builds school spirit and morale tremendously. Cheerleaders are involved, and possibly the school band. Young people need salutary pastimes—which involve them, and utilize their time, as well. These are safe channels for their emotions. Ballplayers can spend hours practicing—hours which they might have spent smoking pot. The needs of adolescents for belonging, for achievment, for status and recognition can be met extremely easily and pleasurably by being part of a team.

If you prefer, or if there are no other schools in your area, intraschool teams may be established. It is possible to set up a league of teams within your school—modeling it, perhaps, on the leagues in professional sports. In this way a number of games may be played, with championship as the major goal.

Girls' teams, as well as boys', should be established—basketball and volleyball being some of the possibilities. Girls need this type of team activity as much as boys. They also require physical exercise, and, in this form, it is fun as well as functional. However, if such teams are established try to keep in mind, at all times, the fact that these are young ladies who are playing. Their dress and behavior should not be similar to that of young men. While the girls' team may play against the boys', we do not believe this should be fostered. Nor should young ladies be forced to play as hard. The idea of a number of teams playing in a league situation is a good possibility.

One of the best devices for raising morale, for building rapport and comaraderie and for sheer good fun, is a faculty-student ballgame. Be it baseball or basketball, it's guaranteed to win friends and influence people. This can be used, too, as a fund-raising device—for it has been our experience that both pupils and teachers will want to participate, and will attend. Use as many teachers in the game as possible—and include the most staid and the most dignified. Somehow the sight of the gentleman who is always perfectly attired, in sweat shirt and shorts, makes him more human—as far as his pupils are concerned. Be careful, however, to make sure that no adult who is relatively inactive and does not get much exercise gets involved in any game which might cause him to have a heart attack. As an added fillip—use teacher cheerleaders!

The teams are an excellent area in which to involve the parents and other members of the community. This may be done in a number of ways. Sponsors of the team, who help bear the financial burden, are invited to all games, given places of honor, introduced to the spectators, and in general made to feel important. They may be invited to watch the teams practice, to talk with the coaches, and to travel with the team to games away from the home field. We know of a retired gentleman who built a satisfying life for himself as a sponsor of his local high school's teams—switching with the seasons from football to basketball to baseball.

It is possible to utilize the talents of members of the community by permitting them to serve as assistant coaches, and/or business managers. Guest speakers with experience in the field may also be invited to discuss their personal experiences with the team. Because two heads are better than one, and because thought begets thought, this technique has value. It also gives status to the team members, so that the relationship may become a symbiotic one.

Mothers may be asked to help make uniforms for the cheerleaders. These are not difficult to sew, and add a great deal to the school's prestige at game time.

Fund raising is another area in which parents and the community may be involved. The concept must be presented to them that the teams help keep their young people occupied and interested. Most of all the teams keep them out of trouble because the youngsters are so busy they have no time for harmful experimentation. With this idea in mind, the parents will surely not be antagonistic to the school's efforts to build successful teams, and, in most cases, will do as much as they can to build a successful program. We have said before, the busy youngster usually stays out of trouble. When he is a member of a team he is relating to others, not isolating himself from them. So often we find it is the isolate who, because he is unhappy, tries drugs. He is alone, and miserable, and seeks the lift they are supposed to give him. The child who belongs to a team has friends and companions. Usually he has a good relationship with the coach of the team. He must, because of the rules of the team, do his school work. Because of the need for physical fitness, he must stay in training, and this, too, keeps him out of trouble. When explained to the parents and the community on this basis, emphasizing the point that athletics are a wholesome and salutary outlet for the children's emotions, and will possibly preclude their participation in anti-social and un-wholesome activities, how can they be anything but enthused and cooperative?

HOW TO DEVELOP A
GOOD PUBLIC RELATIONS PROGRAM

A person who knows the skills involved in attaining good public relations is needed. The activities of the teams need publicity, and such a person should be asked to act as press secretary. His (or her) function is to report to the local newspaper all news of the teams. This should include human interest stories, as well as the results of games. Very often newspapers are in need of copy, and willing to carry articles about teams, or about team members or coaches. In addition to this, the school newspaper should feature column upon column of information in this vein. It is a fine medium to bring to the attention of the local people, the athletes in their midst. (It should run articles in regard to academic, creative and other talents, as well.) Good publicity is a tremendous morale builder.

Contacting the local radio and television stations sometimes results in interview programs, which add, too, to school spirit. Should any of your students, faculty or community members appear on either radio or television, we suggest you give them full advance publicity, for, quoting an old adage, "Why hide your light under a barrel?" This sort of publicity benefits everyone—and harms no one.

As many children as possible should be involved in this team program. We have mentioned the business staff, which performs many important functions. In addition to the cheerleaders, a "boosters" group may be created among the girls. Boosters may, if desired, wear costumes similar to the cheerleaders. They may or may not appear on the playing field, but by sitting together in the stands, waving banners and cheering enthusiastically, they play a part, too, in achieving victory. Mascots may be selected from among the youngest and smallest members of the student body. (It is important, however, to remember these children should only be chosen if they are not sensitive about their small size.) Photographers, from among the students, may take action pictures of the games.

One aspect of the team program in the high schools which cannot be overlooked is the tremendous number of opportunities which may be offered to some of the athletes (and musicians) in the form of college scholarships. These young people have skills which the colleges need—and are willing and anxious to obtain through the awarding of scholarships. Many, many cases of this nature are known of—and no secret is made of the situation. Nor is there anything wrong in this—for skills of all kinds are purchased, in every field of endeavor. By training football players, we help to prepare these boys for possible careers after college, as well.

The scholarships often help the youngster who might otherwise never attend college, for lack of funds. They make it easier for those who would otherwise have financial problems. By helping our youngsters to get scholarships, we do them and their families a tremendous service. Let us not minimize this.

The Tutorial Program 6

Since the primary task of the school is to educate all of the children, and since not every child learns at the same rate, or is working at the same level, there are times when youngsters require help with their school work. This may be a temporary condition, or a permanent one. The child may be bright in one subject, but have difficulty with another. He may need repetition in order to grasp certain ideas. He may be a slow learner, requiring much interpretation, variation, careful reiteration and reteaching on the part of the teacher. A youngster may have been out of school for a period of time, and missed the work which was done while he was away. He may have forgotten the material he learned the previous year. He may have serious learning problems which require a great deal of individual instruction. For all of these reasons, a tutorial program is a virtual necessity. It can be the most important aspect of school to some children. To others it can offer the assistance which parents are often incapable of giving. Children desperately need to "do something right," and it may be the tutorial program which enables them to do so.

TUTORS FOR THE PROGRAM

There are a number of ways in which you can find teachers for this program. We will list several—and you may choose one or two of these—or combinations.

1. Teachers may be asked to teach in the tutorial program or may be scheduled for this. In some communities as part of his regu-

lar day, the teacher is programmed for an extra period during which he does tutoring.

2. Student teachers who are assigned to a school may be asked to take part in the tutorial program for the valuable experience of working in a one to one relationship with individual children.
3. Parents and members of the community who are anxious to help the children, and who have the ability to do so, might be enlisted to take part in the tutorial program.
4. College students attending colleges in the area may be hired to tutor. This is particularly valuable for them if they plan to become teachers or eventually parents.
5. The older pupils in the school may work with the younger ones, often providing very satisfying experiences for both groups.

On an Open School Night, one of the authors was approached by a little girl and her mother.

"Is Lisa your daughter?" the woman asked.

"Yes. Of course. Do you know Lisa?"

"Oh, yes. We want to thank you."

"For what?"

"Lisa taught Peggy, here, to read."

This mother was referring to the tutorial program—and what is most noteworthy is that, at the time, Peggy was in the second grade, and Lisa was in the sixth.

We must stress one point. With the exception of the regular teachers on the school staff, any other tutors must be trained by the professional teachers—and given specific methods and even materials to use. It would be far worse for a tutor to confuse a child than to not tutor him at all. This is particularly true when there are a number of methods possible. The so-called "new Math" comes to mind immediately. If the tutor uses a method different from the one the classroom teacher uses, this can really be detrimental to the child's learning. In any tutoring program, it is necessary to have briefing sessions, and to make sure that each tutor consults with the child's teacher to find out what skills the child lacks, and how the teacher has been teaching them to date. This does not imply that the teacher dictates to the tutor. Nor does it mean the tutor cannot use his own ingenuity. But there must be some collaboration, so that each knows what the other is doing.

Every tutor should also report back to the classroom teacher periodically, too, giving the progress and listing the areas in which he considers the child needs further help. By this method far more can be accomplished than if each person working with the child is proceeding independently, without the knowledge of what specifically the other is teaching.

This type of tutorial program enables the school to really individualize instruction. Each child can be taught what he needs, and is not restricted by the rest of the class. Because there are children who require much repetition before they can learn certain concepts, tutoring is ideal. The tutor can repeat and reiterate, time and again, without boring the remainder of the class. It is hoped he will be able to utilize some new approaches, and even new techniques, being sure these fit the needs of the child. For example, there are many youngsters who cannot grasp the concept of the complete sentence, and write run-on sentences time and again. It seems that no textbook can show them of what a sentence consists, and when it becomes run-on. But a tutor, using the child's own writing, and his own compositions, can often bring this home to the youngster as he discusses the long list of thoughts in the child's sentences.

Very often even a skillful teacher cannot spend the time it takes to break down certain learning barriers which have developed. We do not promise that a tutor can, but we feel that many, many times this is possible. In many situations the establishment of a one-to-one relationship is the most important aspect of the tutoring program. The child knows that, for the time he is allotted, he receives the full attention of another human being. There are children who crave this, who need it, and who will benefit far more from it than would seem possible. For youngsters from large families, as many of our disadvantaged children are, this quiet contact with another human being, a person who is interested in him, can have far more value than is readily discernible. There are many children who do not know words, and whose lack of the basic communication skills will haunt them throughout their school lives. The tutor, by his very speech and use of vocabulary, can assist the child in this very important area. Then, too, his sympathetic feeling for the child (which is bound to be communicated to the youngster, if the feeling is genuine) will have far-reaching salutary effects upon the little one, not only during his school life, but also extending into his adulthood. How many of us have gained confidence and strength that was born of a one-to-one relationship with an understanding teacher or a fine tutor.

Choose the staff for your tutorial program with the greatest of care. If the one-to-one relationship is to have significance to the child, the tutor must have a feeling for children, as well as be able to convey knowledge. Not only with disadvantaged, but with all children, the development of rapport is important, for no young person, growing up, can have too much of this form of communication. How can a child freely discuss his learning problems if he feels a barrier between himself and his tutor? Perhaps this is why older children can often effectively teach younger ones.

—Official Photograph, Board of Education, City of New York

A ONE-TO-ONE RELATIONSHIP BRINGS THEM CLOSER TOGETHER

We have just mentioned children's problems. To many adults they may seem of little import and in far too many situations they are ignored. Yet how can we ignore them, if they are troubling the child and thereby interfering with the learning. We know of one little girl with a terrible problem—or so she thought. She could not tell her left hand from her right until a bright student teacher showed her the letter "L" formed by her left hand. (The thumb and forefinger, with the palm facing down, form the "L".) End of problem. But, more important, the child learned it was not a difficult thing to solve problems and that other difficulties could probably be handled equally easily, provided he made his problems known, and discussed them. It is also noteworthy to mention that it should be emphasized to the child that he should feel free to discuss his problems with his teacher or his tutor, and that he will be happier if he does. It is far better to do this than to let the problems linger and rankle in his mind.

It is exceedingly important that the children see that they are benefiting, for if they are to actively participate they must be motivated—and the best motivation achieved is when the child sees results. We suggest that, at the end of each session, the tutor summarize by asking, "What did you learn today?" Get the child to answer in terms of specifics. Or the tutor may say, "Today we worked on _____. I think you understand this concept better than you did when we started. What do you think? Which area is clearer?"

Another point which will strengthen the tutorial program is the communication between the tutor and the classroom teacher. For, as the latter sees improvement and comments upon it, he reinforces the tutor's position in the eyes of the student.

DETERMINING THE TUTORIAL PROGRAM
FOR YOUR SCHOOL

A survey of the school records of standardized reading test results will reveal the amount of tutoring time which should be devoted to reading. We believe this cannot possibly be over-emphasized. There is absolutely no doubt in regard to the vast effect the ability to read has on the academic future of every child. The child who cannot read is often the one who ultimately drops out of school. His future is clouded from the first grade and he is more than likely to develop inferiority complexes.

Let us think about the vast areas of knowledge from which he is excluded throughout his life merely because he has not mastered reading techniques. He may be a person with a normal or even a high degree of intelligence, and may even have a thirst for learning, but, if through some intellectual mishap, or some mental or physical disease, he has been unable to master the art of reading, consider how handicapped he will be throughout his entire life. What intellectual pleasures will be denied him! What opportunities for employment will be impossible for him to achieve. In a word, his entire life might be blighted because he has not learned to read.

We would strongly suggest, therefore, that the tutorial program first serve those children who have reading problems. Every boy or girl who shows reading retardation should be recommended for tutoring—even if this is the only subject which will be offered, and even if it means to the second and third graders. They must be helped to see just how important it is that they learn to read, and possibly, in this situation, they will actually master reading.

If, however, the students are unable or unwilling, or simply do not come, or if sufficient funding is not available, we suggest you determine the subject areas in one of two ways. You may either send out questionnaires to the teachers asking them how many children require tutoring in a specific area, or you may ask the parents in which subjects they would like to have tutoring available for their children. There are advantages for both of these, and we prefer a combination of the two because the parental influence can be most important in getting children to participate. We would suggest you send a notice to the parents saying, "We are planning to establish a tutorial program after school. Do you feel you would like your child to participate? From our records we believe he (or she) could benefit from this kind of special help in _____." (Teacher would fill in the subject.) "Are you interested in sending him for this help? Please answer below and return this notice as soon as possible. Thank you."

Based on the replies you receive, you can determine which subjects you will offer.

How are children chosen for the tutorial program? Without doubt the child who is aware of the need, himself, will benefit most. The classroom teacher who can deftly steer a child toward seeking assistance does him a great favor. However, this must be done without embarrassing the youngster in any way. Other means are through parental intervention. A note on the report card, a letter to the parents, or a telephone call to them may all be used. Parents may be invited, too, to observe the program, with the hope they will be able to sell it to their children. But no child should be made to feel inadequate because he is receiving additional teaching. On the other hand, he should be praised for being mature enough to be aware of his inadequacies, and seeking to remedy the condition.

As part of the tutorial program, we suggest you establish a place for children to do their homework where they can seek aid if they require it. The library is often used for this purpose, but it need not be. Another room may be set up. More than one student has told us that he found it difficult to study because he felt lonely. The tutorial program brings children together, and loneliness and its accompanying feeling of depression are defeated. There are children who have no one at home to help them clarify a question or solve a problem, and who need this help—inconsequential as it may seem. For these children there is a psychological boost, as well. We have seen the "light dawn" in a child's face as he realized "I before E except after C" is a rule which really works. We personally recall being impressed by a young tutor who knew what a "cyst" was.

The library is an excellent place for research but not for tutoring. The sound of normal voices which should and must be part of tutoring can be distracting to others. If the library must be used, section it off so that part of it will remain quiet.

THE TIME FOR TUTORING

Your tutorial program may take place during the school day, after school or both. It may involve a few children or a few hundred, but it should be established to meet the actual needs of the children.

If your school has the space for it, tutoring may be done effectively during the lunch period. However, each tutor must have a quiet place in which to work—and that cannot possibly be the school cafeteria. More than one tutor can use a classroom, but

An Opportunity To Serve

by Joanna Davis

At 8:A.M. Mondays, Wednesdays and Thursdays there is a coaching session in the Old Lunch Room. At that time 9th grade students help other seniors in 9th year math. It's all quite enjoyable as well as beneficial.

The "tutors" are members of a club called the "Future Teacher's Club" which meets with Mrs. Perrin in the O.L.R., Tuesdays at 8: A.M. The main purpose of this club is to give hints on teaching to any ninth-grade boy or girl who thinks he might choose teaching as a career. Of course, this is not a binding choice. A "future teacher" of 1967 may be President by 1997.

Mrs. Perrin points out many teaching opportunities for Castle Hill-ites:

1) The A.M. Coaching Program
2) Helping in 127's After-School Study Center.
3) Belonging to the Junior Volunteer Corps.

Besides these activities, the Future Teacher's Club is in charge of the drives that are held during the school year — the clothing drive, the Christmas drive and many others.

Students who sign up for this last activity are assigned to an elementary school in their neighborhood. There they are teacher assistants one day a week, from 3:15 to 5: P.M., in that school's afternoon program.

This year, the Future Teacher's Club plans to sponsor a child from overseas. Each member will pay a quarter a month. It is hoped that each succeeding club will continue to aid the child.

If you want to get a taste of what it feels like to be on the "other side of the teacher's desk," 9th graders, come out and join our Future Teachers Club!

—*Excerpt from* Castle Hill Currents, *Newspaper of Junior High School 127, Bronx, New York* limit the number in order to keep the room reasonably quiet. We have found, for example, that a group of adult volunteers, working with the children in a one-to-one relationship in one classroom during the school day has been very successful. They work only on reading, with youngsters whose retardation is approximately one or two years, and they work eminently successfully—one dozen tutors and one dozen children in a single classroom.

The system of the older children tutoring the younger is more effective during the day—it seems that both tutor and student are a bit reluctant to remain after school. If study periods are included in the children's schedule this is an excellent use for them. If not, you may wish to allow children to miss certain minor subjects to obtain the assistance they need. This must be handled deftly, for teachers of minor subjects are often sensitive to "slights" and this should be avoided whenever possible.

If the program is to be held after school, we suggest some food be made available—either by giving or selling it to the children. It need be nothing more elaborate than milk and cookies, or ice cream, but it should be rich in energy. By the time three o'clock has rolled around, most children are low in blood-sugar, and need a snack. This is one reason they come home from school ravenously hungry. If we expect them to benefit from tutoring we should provide them with food which produces energy.

We must consider, too, giving them a fifteen or twenty minute break after school so that they have time to stretch, to talk with their friends and to relax before they settle down to work again. The rest period, and the food will refresh and refuel them—so that they will be more comfortable physically, and therefore, more able to learn.

THE ADMINISTRATOR
OF THE TUTORIAL PROGRAM

The teacher or the supervisor placed in charge of the tutorial program should be a person who is interested in the welfare and development of children, and a good administrator. It is his task to select the teachers, to arrange for the places where they will meet with the children they are tutoring, and to supply them with materials which they will use. It is he who should determine, working with the principal (if the principal is not taking charge himself) which teachers or tutors will work with which children, and it is in this area that he can be most successful. If he knows that there are personality problems, and these so often accompany learning problems, he must be very careful to find the appropriate person, one who can empathize with the specific child, and can be of help to him. He cannot be rigid, and must be willing to make changes when they are necessary. It is his task to recognize which teacher is most skillful in which area, and will be able to convey the most to a particular child. He will have budgetary problems to cope with, as well, and the inevitable paper work which accompanies such a position. But it is important that he be the type of person who can handle these problems without becoming discouraged. He needs, too, to be able to awaken confidence in the children, so that they will confide in him if they find they are not getting as much help from the tutorial program as they should. The door to his office should be open, and he should be very much a part of the scene if he is to function effectively. He should speak to the boys and girls receiving tutoring often, constantly evaluating their efforts. He may wish to have attendance taken on a formal or informal basis, but he should know which children are attending, and if any one drops out of the program, he should try to determine why this is so, and prevent it. He must have his finger on the pulse of the situation at all times.

INNOVATIONS IN TECHNIQUES

Tutoring is an excellent opportunity for the teacher, if she is doing the tutoring herself, or for any other tutor to try some of the new teaching methods and devices which are available. For example, the new programmed materials might add the interest, and entice the imagination of a child who has been apathetic in the classroom. The whole approach used by the teaching machines can capture the child who has been "turned off" by the books he has been reading, or the materials the teacher has used. Learning may be made more of a game by the use of these devices. Indeed, any game which a teacher can create can be utilized effectively in the tutoring situation. Workbooks, too, can add to the tools which can be tried. These, however, should be used with not a grain of salt, but a teaspoonful, for they often give the child the impression they are merely busy work, and he will resent this. But specific pages, preferably removed from the book and given to the child, accompanied with an explanation for the specific reason they are being used can be very effective.

The basis of the teaching machine, and of programmed learning is a simple one. The child answers a question. He moves his answer sheet, and finds the answers and alternatives. If he was correct, he is instructed to go on to an indicated page. If he was not, he goes on—but to a different page, where the material is repeated, but in another form. The constant movement and the alternatives and choices offered to him will intrigue the child, and whet his appetite. Most important, if he is correct he will get immediate satisfaction from seeing the words, "That is correct. Now proceed to page XYZ." Frustration is thus defeated and success encouraged. The child's confidence is nurtured. A tutor can utilize these principles, experiment with them, and create his own programmed learning. He may then work with it with individual children.

Tutors may write their own stories, rexograph them, and use them for the teaching of reading, or for language arts. They may also create miniature experience charts, written from the child's words, of happenings which affected him. He will be far more interested in reading them than any book imaginable, and this is feasible in the one-to-one situation.

The tape recorder is another favorite of the children, and can be utilized, for this reason, with very favorable results. They love to work with it—so that, if the tutor is able to weave it into his lessons, he will find it will motivate the children. Reading into a microphone is far more exciting than just reading to another person.

Personal viewers, used with filmstrips, are practical devices which help any tutor. They combine color and interest—if good filmstrips are chosen, and give the child the opportunity to have them "all to himself."

In teaching subjects other than reading, use the printed page while working with the individual child. The tutor should utilize many books and printed sources. It should not be a period of solely verbal communication. The reasons for this are twofold. Children need experiences in reading, and should get some of them during this time—for they have the assistance of a teacher who will help them to learn as much as possible from the printed page. Secondly, reading skills can be taught very effectively at the same time as other subject matter. Science and social studies easily fit into this category. The tutor has an excellent opportunity to help build a familiarity and a comfort with books, magazines, newspapers and with the resources available in the library. The learning process in human beings has long been the basis for a great deal of study. It is known that a huge amount of learning is through reading, far more than through listening. The child should be encouraged to read silently and then the tutor should draw out what he has learned by questioning him. The best tutoring is to have the child actually doing something valuable as much of the time as possible. Busy work is, of course, to be avoided, but interesting exercises to reinforce learning are very worthwhile. However, the tutor must often check by asking the child, "Do you understand?" and reteaching anything with which the child is having difficulty.

ENRICHMENT

Another aspect of a tutorial program which can and should be included is the enrichment program. There are many students, for example, who would request typing, if it were offered, but this is often not possible during the school day. However, if it can be given as part of the tutorial program, many of them will find time after school to take it. This skill has become increasingly valuable to youngsters in high school and college, and while it may easily be studied at home, offering it to them in school is a definite accommodation, and one which the parents very actively seek. Furthermore, the children definitely enjoy learning to use the typewriter. We would suggest that, in an area where most of the children will be attending college, typing is a most worthwhile addition to the tutorial program. Many young people who do not need assistance will be interested in developing speed and accuracy, for they realize how valuable this skill is, both while they are attending school, and during the summers if they wish to seek employment. In connection with this, another subject worthy of consideration is a form of shorthand which uses letters rather than symbols, and which may be learned quickly. This, too, is useful in college, and for the boy or girl who wishes to have some skill to offer an employer during the summer or part time, after school.

In many schools courses are offered to help the child choose a college or take examinations for college entrance. The latter involve review work in mathematics, and a good deal of material in vocabulary and reading skills. These help the child to prepare for his future in a practical way.

However, enrichment, unfortunately, must come after the bread and butter tasks, the reading and arithmetic. These must still form the basic part of the tutorial program. But, if funds are not a problem, art, home economics, industrial arts, and sports may all be included. These are not club situations, but bona-fide classes, which will hopefully have relatively few pupils in a class, and which will be able to proceed at the children's pace, and include the materials they wish to cover. Individual attention is the keynote of any tutorial work or course.

PARENTAL INVOLVEMENT

Any program will be more likely to prove successful if the parents are aware of it, and even more so, if they are enthused about it and involved in it. In a tutoring program, parents can be of assistance in many ways. They should surely be informed, if they have not already been told of the need their child has for tutoring. This is important because quite often the parents must be reminded that the child lacks certain skills and needs help. A conference between parents, tutor and teacher can be very valuable for motivation of the child, and of the parents. It is also a way of giving the child attention, which he may be very actively seeking.

Encourage the parents to communicate with the tutor, and to

discuss the child and his learning problems with him. Often this teacher is in a position to help. He is able to teach study skills, for example, when necessary. He can introduce the child to the library and to research. He can help the child to improve his spelling or his writing, and even his handwriting. This opportunity for truly individualized attention should not be missed.

SUMMARY SHEET

A summary sheet will help your tutors by bringing their attention to certain factors. It should be filled out every term, and should be kept on file. It should list *for each child* the following information:

1. The child's name, his homeroom class and teacher.
2. The subject in which he is to be tutored.
3. (From his subject teacher) The specific areas to be worked on first, i.e. Math—division of fractions. Science—scientific method of reasoning. English—Run-on sentences.
4. The method the tutor used and found to be most effective in teaching this child this skill.
5. The child's judgment of progress made.
6. The tutor's judgment of progress.
7. Is there a need for further tutoring? If so, in what areas?
8. How can this child be made to feel comfortable? What approach succeeded with him?
9. The home situation: Are parents cooperative? Did they attend the conference? Did they assist with homework?
10. What further can be done to help this child achieve?

Guidelines for the
Operation of an Effective
Evening School Program

7

By operating an evening school program as part of the extra-curricular activities of the school, it is possible to serve the adults as well as the children of the community. Indeed, evening school courses are able to serve many different purposes. For the pupils, they can be the opportunity to take subjects which are not offered to them in their regular curriculum. The youngsters are able to enrich their lives, by a study of music or of art, of crafts or typing. They can study the subjects they are anxious to learn, and consequently will do well in those subjects. In most schools a young person cannot study chess or Chinese in the course of a regular day, but he may be able to in evening school.

Adults, parents and other members of the community are encouraged to attend classes, as well. The program should be set up to meet their needs, as well as those of the children, for if the school is really to serve the community, and be in tempo with the times, then it must offer something to everyone.

MEETING THE NEEDS OF BOYS AND GIRLS

There are many courses which your students cannot fit into their programs, but which they may wish to study. Typing and shorthand fall into this category, and if you offer the type of short-hand which uses letters instead of symbols, they can learn it in a relatively short time. While this will not enable them to take two-hundred words a minute, it will suffice for use in college, and in many business offices.

There are many art and music courses, as well as home economics and industrial arts in which the youngsters are interested. Photography is very popular, particularly if there is a darkroom and equipment available to the students.

Courses which prepare your young people for summer work have practical worth—filing, simple bookkeeping and using office machines for example. A course in lifesaving, too, can serve them well. We will list a number of courses later in this chapter.

MEETING THE NEEDS OF ADULTS IN THE COMMUNITY

For an effective program, the school administration must study the community and its needs and determine, specifically, what these needs are. This may be done through discussion with members of the Parent Association, through personal interviews, through questionnaires and surveys, and especially through meetings with those people who indicate interest in registering for the courses. In those communities in middle income areas the subjects requested will be markedly different from those needed in an area of economically disadvantaged persons. In the former there will be those individuals seeking hobbies and enrichment, as well as those seeking skills which they plan on using to increase their earning capacity.

The evening school also offers a place for sociability, and socializing is one of the very important reasons for their popularity with many young, unattached adults. We do not mean to imply there is anything wrong with this. On the contrary, it is our feeling that this can be one of its most valuable contributions to modern life.

For many, many years the night school served immigrants who came to our shores, and who needed to learn to read and write English. Many of them attended school to better themselves after they had finished their day's work. We recall the remarks made by a dear lady, in her late sixties, who had just married her third husband and was anxious to impress him: "You have to learn English," she said to him. "You just have to learn to speak English." She continued in this vein for fully ten minutes. Her final statement was, "You must learn English. After all, we *mangle* with the best people."

If there are residents of your area who need such courses, should you not offer them at hours which are convenient? Should you not make "English for foreigners," as valuable as possible? And should it not be called by a more inviting name, such as "English for today's world"?

Today there are thousands of people who attend evening school for less serious reasons. Perhaps it is for enrichment—for cultural courses, such as art or music appreciation, for modern dance, or for Yoga. We are finding that many individuals are anxious to become participants rather than on-lookers, and learning to play a guitar or speak Russian or Swahili is *doing,* rather than observing.

In the areas where there are many financially disadvantaged people, the needs are, of course, different. Here we are more apt to find requests for the skill courses or for remedial work. Courses enabling the person to take an equivalency examination to get a high school diploma are important, and should be offered. Most colleges, as part of their entrance requirements, ask for a course in high school algebra, and offering such a course can be a real service to the people of the community.

Courses might be offered to help people whose education has been meagre, to develop their backgrounds. Dr. Gene Fusco, in *Improving Your School Community Relations,* Prentice-Hall's Successful School Administration Series, states, "The vital importance of the home in shaping the educational attitudes and behavior of the child is generally recognized. What happens or does not happen to the child at home largely determines what kind of pupil he will be in school. . . . In light of the great weight of evidence that the intellectually and culturally restricted home life of the socially disadvantaged children places heavy obstacles in their path for succeeding in school, many believe that the inner-city schools should make extraordinary efforts to assist parents in overcoming such obstacles." What better way could this be done than by offering courses, at their neighborhood schools, at times when they are able to take them, to upgrade their own education?

Another segment of the population we should try to serve is the young marrieds-new parents group. Both men and women in this age group often need creative outlets, for their lives can become drudgery without some form of self-expression or growth endeavor. Courses in evening school can fulfill these needs, can offer an evening out, and can provide a place to meet people with similar interests. For young homemakers, work in decorating or sewing, entertaining on a budget, or antique hunting in thrift shops can prove invaluable. For the young men, refinishing furniture, doing simple household repairs, gardening or uncomplicated automobile repairs can prove to be heaven-sent. Young parents appreciate such subjects as baby or child care, or child psychology. These young adults, whose education often terminated with high school, should have opportunities to find courses geared for them, at this particular time in their lives.

It is difficult to find ways to communicate with this age group. It is surely not too effective to send notices home with your students because they will, in most probability, not reach them. If your community has many people falling into this category, publicize the program in the local newspaper, or send notices to graduates of the school.

Evening school should be open to everyone and everyone should be encouraged to participate. The program should be open to girls and boys, mothers and fathers, and grandmothers and grandfathers. There should be something for everyone, regardless of age. This is one means the school has for serving the community, and for serving it well. We are living in an age of self-expression, and of self-development, and it behooves us to help people to "do their own thing." Where should a person turn, if he wishes to learn a skill, or develop an ability, but to the school? By keeping our fees low, by offering scholarships to those who cannot afford even these, and by adopting the attitude that we are in business to serve not only the children but the adults of the community as well, we insure our development as an institution of the future, not of the past.

How can you decide which programs to offer?

It is absolutely essential to determine which courses the people want, which they need, and above all, which they will attend. If we are asked for a course in the collection of Chinese pottery of the fifteenth century, and enough people register for it, then we should offer it. It is as simple as that!

There are a number of methods to determine the curriculum offerings:

Discuss the matter with the executive board of the Parents' Association, and then with the entire body. Get their reactions, and have them suggest courses to be offered to adults as part of the curriculum of the evening school. Find out, too, if they will permit their children to participate, and if so, which subjects to offer to them. As we have said, the cooperation of parents is vital to the success of any endeavor.

Announce the program to your boys and girls, inviting them to enroll. (Seventh grade children are the youngest we would recommend.) It is possible you may wish to limit this program to high school students. Get their reactions. Commitments, signed by their parents, should be obtained while you are in the planning stage of the program.

Send out flyers, through the mails, asking people to indicate those courses in which they are interested, from the list given, or to write in the names of those they would like to take. (This is primarily useful to get your program started. Once it is initiated this may be repeated, but it is not necessary to do so.)

Notices may be sent home with the children attending your school to their parents and neighbors, or you may advertise the program in the local and school newspapers. Posters may be displayed in the community—in stores, and public places. In every letter, poster and such, invite the people to come in, to discuss their needs with the director of the evening school. The best type of contact is the personal one, and this should be fostered, particularly if the program is just getting off the ground, and you are anxious to have it get a good start.

Send speakers to community and church groups—to introduce the program, and to ask for suggestions. Listen to these carefully. They can serve as important clues for running a successful program.

You will need someone, usually the director, to do the public relations work involved, to keep the community informed of the work being done, and the offerings of the evening school. This aspect is often neglected, and this is a serious error, because many valuable programs fall by the wayside because of the lack of public support. An uninformed public cannot possibly offer support, and it is your task to make and keep it informed.

The evening school program may be included in your school budget, and courses offered at no cost, or there may be a fee charged. Try to keep these fees to an absolute minimum. If a course requires materials, the cost may be added on, or the pupils encouraged to purchase their own in the local stores. Sometimes it is necessary for the teacher to do this purchasing, for the items needed may be rather difficult to obtain. When possible, try to apply for federal funding. There are often funds available, and surprisingly, they go begging for lack of requests, incredible as this may sound. We urge you to make inquiries—you may find your time exceedingly well spent. And now, more and more, as the government becomes involved in the affairs of the disadvantaged, funds become accessible, and you may discover that your school program fits the specifications. The government's designation of poverty areas may surprise you.

You may wish to develop a sliding scale of fees, charging more for certain courses than for others. It would almost be necessary to charge more for a course with six students in it than one with sixteen. We would hope that the classes be kept to no more than twenty students whenever possible. This is essential in the skills courses. Large groups can function well in physical fitness, for example, but not so well in a class in golf instruction, for the criticism of the individual is an important phase of the latter, while not of the former.

Each course should be taught by a teacher who treats every student with dignity and respect. Teachers must realize that their students may be physically unable to do a great deal of work, for most of them will have labored at their occupation all day. In courses such as "beginning reading," or "Preparation for Citizenship," the role of the teacher is of the utmost importance, for he or she often becomes the person this student emulates. The teacher has the responsibility of making this student feel important, worthwhile, and an asset to our nation. It is a great deal to ask, but it should and must be done.

CHOOSING THE DIRECTOR AND STAFF
OF THE EVENING SCHOOL PROGRAM

The choice of the personnel for the evening school program can make the difference between its success and failure. It is a simple matter to say the teachers should have empathy, verve and enthusiasm, and it is of prime importance that you find such people. They must, above all, be good teachers, willing and anxious to teach. They need not be professionally trained, but they should have a grasp of their subject matter, and of the manner in which to teach it. We have seen artists, very skillful and talented people, who make undesirable teachers because they do not teach, but merely criticize. Each teacher should have his course of study—whether he maps it out, or if it is given to him is relatively unimportant. What is important is that he use this as a guide, but then vary it to meet the needs of the members of the class. Let us say that one particular group is a sewing class. Each student should be able to make garments which she wishes to work on. No one should be compelled to make an apron or a skirt. She should be taught the skills she needs, guided and advised, and then permitted to work on projects of her own choosing. We personally know of one woman who registered in a painting class, being aware of the fact that she was unable to draw, but hoping she would be able to paint, in spite of this. She had ideas about color, line, and composition which she wanted to try to put on canvas. The teacher placed a flower pot with greenery against a drape and said, "Sketch this, and then paint it." The teacher then proceeded to walk around the room, making comments on the work being done in the class. They were suggestions for improving the work, which suited some of the other students in the class—but, for a novice, this was very discouraging. Two weeks of classes of this sort, and the student found excuses to miss several sessions, and then it was "impossible" to return. The teacher was critical, but criticism is not teaching. She should have taught the fundamentals of oil painting.

Evening school classes should be markedly different from regular classes. They should be made as relaxed as possible, and relevant to the students' expectations. Very often in a course of this type, it is a good idea for the teacher to ask those enrolled in the course, what they expect to learn from it. Then, from the replies, a curriculum may be structured. This, too, should be flexible, so that it may be changed at any time the teacher or students deem it necessary. Above all, everyone who is taking courses in evening school should feel he is getting a great deal from them—for they require time and special effort on his part.

Courses should be run on a mature level, even if they are composed solely of young people, or of young people and adults. Students should never be talked down to, or get the impression that this work is, in any way, unimportant. These courses should be almost self-motivated, and the wise teacher will capitalize on this.

Courses should be created as soon as there is a sufficiently large enrollment to make them self-sustaining. When they fill up, more sections should be opened, so that anyone seeking a course in the evening school should be able to get it, if at all possible.

Social Centers

The evening school should have a lounge for coffee breaks, and to serve as a place for meeting people and for socializing. A cafe atmosphere, with small tables, and a coffee pot in one corner of the room makes this easily established, and offers a comfortable place to sit and talk, as well as having coffee.

You may wish to hold a dance once a year, to put out a newspaper or newsletter with accounts of the various activities in the evening school. Evening school should be, above all, a friendly place.

We believe the director should have an open door, so that he may keep in tune with the goings on—and so that he can hear compliments as well as complaints. We have found that negative feelings often find expression but people with positive ones very often neglect to take the trouble to express them. It is the director's task to act as the liaison person between the school and the community. His is the task, too, of supervising the entire endeavor, being sure that he constantly evaluates the activities to determine whether or not they are serving their purposes.

Physical Activities

Physical fitness (exercise program) for men and women.
Dancing—ballroom, discotheque, folk, square.
Yoga.
Golf, bowling, tennis and swimming.
Judo for women, for self-defense.
Karate for men.
Life-saving (Red Cross).
Be sure every student is cleared for these activities by his or her physician.

Cultural Pursuits

Foreign languages—include any language the residents of your area are interested in learning. Many times if the region was settled by a particular group, the subsequent generations do not know the language of their parents and grandparents, and wish to study it. We have seen this to be true of Italian and of Swedish. There is wide interest in Chinese, Russian and Swahili at this time. We would emphasize the necessity to teach languages by the conversational methods used in the special language schools, rather than by the conventional techniques used in many high schools and colleges. Your teachers should have their students speaking phrases the very first evening class meets. They should move along, however, and not get bogged down with the same material again and again, which we have personally seen happen. Simple conversation should be the basis of the course, with an absolute minimum of conjugation, for example. Of course memorization of vocabulary is essential to the mastering of any language, but this, too, should be made as easy as possible, by teaching the words and ideas in context.

Art appreciation—by a study of the works of the masters, and an analysis of styles.

Music appreciation—by an introduction to the works of the great classical composers.

Great literature of the United States or of foreign lands.

Enjoying poetry of the past and of the present.

World history.

Negro history.

Ancient civilizations.

Problems of today's world.

In each of these courses, the teacher must be chosen extremely carefully, and must be someone who loves his subject, as well as being very well versed in it. This love and interest conveys itself to the students, and without it, the tired students attending evening school may become very bored.

Hobby Areas

There are many more hobby areas than we are listing, but these are the most popular.

Painting—using all of the various media—oils, water colors, tempera and acrylic.

Drawing and sketching.

Sculpture—including work in clay, stone and metal.

For each of these fields, consider the need for two groups, beginners and advanced, if there is demand for them. They may not be necessary, but this factor should be taken into consideration.

Etching.

Printing and the graphic arts.

Jewelry making.

Ceramics.

In an entirely different vein, *contract bridge and chess.*

Cooking and entertaining—with special offerings such as French, Italian or Chinese cookery.

Photography—specializing in black and white, or color; stills, slides or movies.

Gardening—outdoor or indoor.

Traveling—where to go, why (what is there to be seen there?); how much will it cost?

Specialized Skills

These areas are such that they will enable the student to learn marketable skills:

Typing.
Stenography.
Bookkeeping.

These courses may be offered to beginners, and there may be a demand for refresher work for those already having learned the skills, but feeling "rusty":

Woodworking.
Antiquing furniture.
Playing a musical instrument—today the guitar is The Instrument. Tomorrow it may be the electric organ. But, in whatever area there is a demand, a course should be offered.
Dress designing and pattern making.
Simple repairs, around the house.
Auto repairs—for both men and women.
Simple carpentry.
Home decorating.
Sewing.
Entertaining on a budget.
Antique hunting in thrift shops.
Furniture refinishing.
Safe boating.
Singing in groups, choirs and choruses.
First aid (American Red Cross course).
Algebra—(Ninth grade math) for people seeking to enter college, and lacking in this specific course.
Preparing for the High School Equivalency Test.

Courses for Enrichment

These courses are appealing to the person who wishes to expand his field of knowledge:

Child Psychology.
Psychology of the normal personality.
Preparing your Income Tax.
New Math for parents.
Understanding the school curriculum.
Helping your child with his school work.
Real Estate investing.
Opening and operating a small business.
Investing in stocks and bonds.
Financing and operating a franchised business.
Law for the layman.
Preparing for Civil Service Examinations (State and federal, too.)
Creative writing, and journalism.

Special Courses for Special Groups

1) Senior Citizens may be interested in any of the courses listed above. In addition, we suggest you offer, especially for them:
Arts and Crafts.
Stamp and coin collecting.
"Let's talk about it"—a discussion club devoted to such topics as books, movies, current events or any subject of interest to the members.
Enjoying your retirement—things to do, places to go; making new friends; doing community service.

2) People new to our shores:
English as your new language (Speaking).
Reading and writing English.
Preparing to become a citizen.
American history for new Americans.

3) For girls and boys:
Baby sitting—the successful completion of this course should be accompanied by a certificate, and by listing in a baby-sitting service.
Improving your reading—for beginners and for advanced students (Separate classes).
Rock and roll music—appreciation and discussion.

Composing music and lyrics.
First aid (American Red Cross course).
Stenography and typing for the college bound.
How to study—and other work skills.
Choosing a career.
Choosing a college.
Preparing for civil, state and federal service.
Skills to prepare for a summer job.

Entertainments— 8
Drama, Concerts
and Much More

A VARIETY OF PROGRAMS

The variety of programs for the purposes of entertainment which may be presented as part of the student activities program is limited only by the imagination of the administrators, faculty members and students. We are going to discuss many types, but we hope you will realize that you can and should take it from there. The originality, the novelty and the uniqueness of your programs will add tremendously to their success, and enjoyment. However, no matter what type of program is decided upon, it is essential that it be as professionally produced and as perfect as possible. This entails a great deal of work—rehearsing, preparing scenery and costumes, and doing the thousand and one tasks necessary. But, by careful planning, by initiating the project well in advance of the production date, and by distributing responsibility, so that no one individual is overburdened, your faculty and students can do so well that parents will say, "This is as good or better than what we've seen on television."

What Types of Productions Can We Put On?

Many schools have drama clubs, and a play, chosen carefully and performed by the club can be a very successful endeavor. This may be a drama or a comedy, a mystery or a narrative; it may be a musical comedy or a story with music.

Concerts are another possible area for production. These may involve choruses and glee clubs, orchestras and bands. They may

—Junior High School 27, Staten Island, New York

"SPRING FESTIVAL" PROGRAM COVER

feature instrumentalists, or singers, groups or small ensembles. An interesting addition which we found effective was the showing of slides, prepared by the students in their art classes, to accompany the musical selections. Changing the lighting effects, which is referred to as "light show" may also be used in this manner.

Modern or interpretive dancing, or ballet, if the youngsters are well trained, can form an entire program, or be part of one combined with a concert. In this way scope is given to the varied talents of the children, and none of the gifts is slighted.

There are other types of programs which are as entertaining, but more unusual—for example, the physical education department can prepare an exciting evening composed of exhibitions of skills, such as precision exercising, rope climbing, cheerleading or shooting baskets. This may be combined with some competitive activities such as relay races, barrel jumping, or sack races, which should be included because they provide so much merriment. Then the evening's entertainment may be concluded with an exhibition of square dancing, and, if you like, you can invite the audience to join in. It goes without saying that if a child has been prohibited by his physician from participating in this type of activity, he must, of course, unfortunately be excluded.

You may have a poetry reading, done in a coffee house atmosphere, or an evening with famous literary figures. The latter would be prepared by an advisor and a staff who have a decided love of literature, and who would choose selections from famous literary works. These should be chosen for their excitement—so that the audience would genuinely enjoy them. Be sure to choose material which the average parent would truly enjoy—not merely selections for the literateur. Despite the fact that these works are read, they require a great deal of preparation, for they should be so familiar to the children that they are almost recited. It is extremely important that a real flow of words is achieved, rather than a halting rendition.

What about a program called "The Magic of Mathematics," with puzzles (for the audience to do), contests to enter, and even instruction in some of the new methods, with which the parents are not usually familiar.

Many high schools, such as Samuel Tilden in Brooklyn, New

York have had, for many years, a program called a "Sing," in which the students in the various grades compete against each other. Their songs and parodies, which they write themselves, carry out a specific theme. Each class uses a different theme for its presentation. This has become an eagerly awaited event each year, with a great deal of excitement focused on it. Costumes and sets have become very elaborate. Originality and perfection of performance are stressed.

Whatever the program is to be, there are a number of considerations which will help to make it successful. Let us discuss some of them:

1) What is the purpose of the program? Is it a vehicle for the children's pleasure? Is it a treat for the parents? Is it necessary to use it to raise funds? Is it being done to raise school morale? Is it an invitation for the community to enter the school and see the work being done? Or is it for all of these—which it very well may be. Whatever the reason or reasons, being aware of them makes it simpler to have an effective program—and a successful one.

2) Will it be financed by the school, or must it be self-supporting or profit making? An entirely different approach is necessary when funding is a problem. This, then, is a factor to be considered. Is there money for costumes, or must they be contributed by parents and other interested parties? Can props be rented? How is the budgeting to be worked out?

3) Who is to decide on the type of program? This decision may be made by the administrative staff, by the faculty, or even by the students. The principal may feel he would like to have a concert, and would consult with the members of the music department. He might consult with his cabinet, and then with department heads. He can, of course, ask for volunteers or for suggestions. However, it is often necessary for this decision to be made unilaterally because if it is bandied about, too often no program results. If a program is needed, if one should be done, we feel it is the principal's role to initiate it. There is often a great deal of work involved, and because many teachers have second jobs or other commitments, they are reluctant to undertake it. He, therefore, may have to consider carefully which department will best be able to put on a program of this nature and which will be able and

willing to do the most professional job. When parents and community members are asked to give of their time, and of their money, they have every right to see something worthwhile.

There are few of us who are parents who have not sat through interminable concerts—as our neophyte pianists performed for five minutes—and we were forced to be part of a captive audience for five hours. Our school programs must bear no resemblance to this. By initiating them well in advance, and by attending several early rehearsals, the principal is able to tell if the production is going to be a worthwhile one. If it isn't, it should be revised until it is. It is unfair, too, to the children to have them work hard on a possible "flop." They almost always put their hearts and souls into such programs, and if the performance proves to be dull or mediocre, the youngsters are crushed. Contrast this with the glow of satisfaction which accompanies a success.

SELECTING A PROPER VEHICLE

There are many ways to insure a worthwhile program. Once the area has been decided upon, a faculty advisor is selected. If a teacher volunteers, he is the person who should be placed in charge. Many of our young teachers have had experience and talent in these areas in summer camps—and this experience can prove to be invaluable. They should be encouraged to volunteer. It is best, too, to find a person who can use this activity as an outlet for his own creativity. The young girl who had studied dramatics in college and had wanted to be an actress, but is now teaching English, can, very often produce a fine play, utilizing the skills she had learned. It is a wholesome channel for her emotions as well as the children's.

It should be the task of the advisor to find the most suitable play, develop the best musical program or work out the most interesting entertainment he can.

We suggest the coming event be announced to the students, via the public address system, the school newspaper and notices to the classes. The advisor should set up a meeting with the students, and work with those who attend. Word should continually be spread, and more and more youngsters will be attracted. They should be asked for suggestions, and these discussed. A list should be drawn up—including the students' suggestions and those of the faculty advisor—and finally a decision made. The children's opinions should get full consideration. If they must be vetoed, valid reasons should be given. The decision, however, should, if at all possible, come from the efforts of both the advisor and the children.

In the case of a play or a musical, choose something with entertainment value, something within the range of the children's and the parents' appreciation and enjoyment—nothing too cryptic, intellectually. The selection should also have social and moral worth. Let us be careful to avoid material which might be distasteful or offensive to the audience. We must be careful not to step on anybody's toes.

The drama has a magnificent potential to unite our people. This is a very desirable antidote for the disruptive forces which exist today. Such plays as "South Pacific," "The Crucible," "Gentlemen's Agreement," or "The Two of Us" embody these objectives. They have entertainment value, social and moral worth, and they tend to bring us together. (What could be more timely?) It is important that as many children as possible be involved: *first,* for the sheer enjoyment the children will derive; *second,* for the beneficial effect it will have in terms of their self-esteem and behavior; *third,* as an outlet for the dramatic talent which so many children possess, thereby nurturing their artistic powers and pride.

Furthermore, the involvement of many children will almost insure a greater audience. The majority of parents are delighted to see their children perform. A musical play or a concert, a dance performance or a physical education demonstration can attract literally hundreds of adults. The evening can prove profitable in enjoyment, and if admission is charged, in raising funds.

To involve children, they may do any of the literally hundreds of tasks involved in producing an entertainment of this sort:

1) The performers and the backstage workers such as those who make the scenery, and who create the costumes. There are those who work the lights, those who act as make-up men, and dressers.

2) The business staff—whose task it is to sell as many tickets as possible.
3) The advertising staff.
4) The youngsters writing and decorating the brochures.
5) The photographers.
6) The ticket-takers and the ushers.
7) Those who do the recording of the songs, and do whatever other tasks are necessary for the success of the production.

We believe stellar roles should be minimized or totally avoided if possible. In this way we will avoid unpleasant comparisons in the roles assigned, and none of the children will be discontented. It is not necessary to compete with Broadway productions.

Let us stress originality and simplicity. The art department can be counted upon to design and make the scenery, and the home economics department, the children and the parents may be asked ɔ do the costumes. We have found the parents most cooperative ι this work.

PREPARING FOR THE PERFORMANCE

It is the duty of the administration to make sure that there are number of teachers asked to assist in the preparation of the proɹuction. It is necessary for more than one teacher to be present while rehearsals are going on. The director should direct, but be assisted in the maintaining of discipline by one or two other teachers, depending upon the size of the production, and the friskiness of the children.

It is important that each little actor or actress understand that, in portraying the character, he should lose his identity and become the person he is portraying. In this way, self-consciousness is automatically shed and his artistic and imaginative powers given full sway. Where the direction is good, a fine rapport between the cast and the director, and among the actors themselves, is achieved. If this is accomplished the resulting play will most probably be a success. The children should be encouraged to help each other in the memorization of their lines.

In the planning, enough rehearsal time should be allotted to avoid as much undesirable pressure as is possible. It is well too, to have a prompter as well as understudies.

If the play selected is currently being shown on stage or screen, it is wise to take the children to see the production first. This will serve as a source of inspiration for their own performance.

If anyone in the school has a parent, relative or friend who is in the theatre, it might be advisable to invite the person in—for suggestions pertaining to the production. He will probably bring with him a theatrical atmosphere which the children will thoroughly enjoy.

ADVERTISING

The success of any venture in the field of entertainment is often measured by the size of the audience. Therefore, every possible avenue for advertising should be employed. For example, the children can write letters to their friends, relatives and to their neighbors inviting them. The principal should put out a newsletter to the parents long in advance, giving the dates of the performances. The art department should do a series of attractive colorful posters, for use around the school, and in the community. They can also prepare handbills to be distributed among the children.

Every child in the school should be encouraged to participate in the advertising of the production, and their ingenuity encouraged. For example, children in costumes can walk through the halls. Samples of some of the finest moments of the play—in the form of "coming attractions"—should be given in the assemblies. Announcements should be made in the cafeteria during lunch hour, and some of the songs might be tape recorded and played.

The school newspaper should carry stories of the production. The local community newspaper should be contacted, and possibly local radio and television stations. Is there a reporter in the community? Perhaps he might be interested in writing an article about the production.

Brochures might be written by the children talented in writing, and distributed to the community. These should be decorated by the youngsters talented in art work. Photos of the production in rehearsal may be displayed in local store windows.

Passes may be given to those shopkeepers who are willing to display the photos, and distribute the brochures.

In this way, there is an interplay of the children's varied talents —writing, art work, or performing. Their business acumen is given a chance to manifest itself and flourish. Cooperative efforts are continuously encouraged, and the result is a tangible production that will delight the children and encourage their creativity and rapport.

Minimize Pressure by Dividing Responsibility

Any entertainment of the type we have been discussing is a tremendous project, and the responsibility for its success should be divided among the members of the faculty. The proclivities of the teachers should be considered. The one with the penchant for art might be in charge of painting the scenery. The wood-working or shop teacher should have the responsibility for building it. The teacher with a gifted pen can supervise the advertising and the printing teacher can produce the handbills and tickets.

The person in charge of the actual production should have assistants assigned to work with him, as has already been suggested. The sewing teachers may be involved in the making of the costumes.

The business aspect of the production should be headed by still another faculty member, whose forte this happens to be. In these ways we combine the efforts and talents of the faculty as well as those of the children. A successful production will prove very gratifying to everyone involved—children, faculty and parents.

The latter may be encouraged to participate in any phase of the production. It is often possible to find someone working in an allied field who will happily contribute his talents to make the evening a "hit."

Parents have, very often, made costumes for us, helped with the scenery and they have worked as dressers and make-up men. They have typed brochures, and even served as assistant directors. If you have worked with the members of the Parent Association, or the Parent Teachers Association, it is a simple matter to request their assistance.

UTILIZING THE CHILDREN'S TALENTS—
AND MAKING THEM HAPPIER

All children, even shy, diffident, unsocial children—not sure of themselves or their abilities, have had their personalities strengthened, and their self-confidence nurtured, by permitting them to appear on the stage. Children can find themselves, through the applause, admiration and approval of their peers, their parents and their teachers. They become more social and find friends through their talent—and school is a happier place for them. Their recognized gift is an Open Sesame not only to the other creative works, but to sociability as well. They are no longer withdrawn, but mingle with the other children of the school, for they have rightfully been given the spotlight. The perceptive teacher is quick to recognize the children's gifts, to encourage them in the development of these talents, and to help to give them full expression and display.

Let creativity and originality be the keynotes of your student activities program. In the entertainment field, you may choose drama, dancing, singing, concerts, poetry readings, health education productions—or any of the many, many skills, which the children so much enjoy displaying. Make your selection worthwhile for its social, moral and entertainment values. Involve as many children as is humanly possible in any of the varied aspects of producing the project. Encourage parental participation, as well. Advertise the production with all the ingenuity the children and faculty can muster. To insure tranquility within the school, divide the responsibilities of the production as fairly as possible among the faculty. Use this program to bring out the talents of those children which might otherwise be ignored.

Above all, make your entertainment truly entertaining. Let's hope you have a block-busting success!

Student Publications— Newspapers, Magazines and Yearbooks

THE CASE FOR STUDENT PUBLICATIONS

There is, indeed, a very strong case in favor of student publications. Let us plead it: All of these publications serve as means of communication within the school—between the students and the staff, and between the students themselves. They also serve as a means of communication with parents and with the community. If our era is new and different, as many claim it is, it is because of the improvement of the communications media. The school needs improved media as well, and one of the most effective ways to improve our communication is through our publications. The individual, his ideas and his thoughts, are given priority in our literary magazines, for example. He is communicating through the written word, as authors and poets have for generations. The artist, too, is communicating through the more-graphic, possibly less-understood medium of his drawings or painting. In our newspapers, it is the latest "happenings" which are communicated and discussed. What problems are on the minds of the editors? There is usually an editorial discussing them. Through the Yearbook, communication with the person of the future is almost guaranteed, for years later yearbooks are picked up and perused. It is for this reason that they must be almost timeless in their approach, and that their contents and their themes never become outdated, but be universal truths which must be as relevant ten years from now, or forty, as they are today.

There are other reasons for the existence of student publications: They raise school morale. They are a source of educational material which skillful teachers of reading and language arts should seize. Children enjoy reading the work of their peers far more than that of adults—for it usually reflects their thinking and their emotions. The language arts teacher may use the publications in another way—as motivation—for the child who does not wish to contribute something for publication in the school magazine or

Teens View Their World

As teenagers we are responsible citizens of our society. Therefore, we have the privilege of expressing our opinions of the world around us.

It is the opinion of many that we teenagers are in the process of rebelling against anything connected with modern adult civilization. Actually, those who rebel are in the minority, composed of beatniks, so-called "artists" and the like. Adults seem to feel that because this minority goes to the extremes of having protests and sit-ins, that a teenager isn't capable of expressing a valid opinion.

We who are connected with the publication of this yearbook feel it is our job to show that we teenagers are and will continue to be responsible citizens who are willing to express constructively our views on the society in which we live.

The Editors

—*Excerpt from Beacon, Magazine of*
Bernstein Junior High School, Staten Island, N. Y.

newspaper is rare indeed. Working on the school publications can provide experiences in the many aspects of publishing. There is far more involved here than writing, as the staff will soon discover. Editing and laying out the material, obtaining advertising, preparing the advertising copy, and obtaining suitable photographs and illustrations are only some of the other tasks involved. School publications give the student interested in a career in writing an opportunity to try his wings, and a tasting sample of work on a magazine or newspaper.

Being on the staff of school publications entails a real job situation in which cooperation with others is essential. This teaches the children many skills they will need as they prepare to enter the world of work.

Lastly they give the child who seeks to express himself an outlet for his thoughts and emotions. They give him a chance to "speak out," and "to tell it like it is."

CLASS NEWSPAPERS AND MAGAZINES

There are other types of publications we feel are important. Class newspapers and magazines, for example, offer many of the advantages mentioned above. There are additional ones, as well. In a class publication every single child should be represented by some piece of work—and it must be something of which he can be proud. When a teacher decides to have a class publication, implicit in this decision is the realization that every boy or girl must be assisted, must be worked with until he or she produces some piece of material worth publishing. It may be a puzzle or a cartoon, an article or a story, an interview or a drawing, but it must be such that the child and his parents can derive pleasure from it.

This publication may reflect all of the subject areas in the curriculum. This is effective in the elementary school, where there is no need to set up restrictions, and where material should flow together. In junior and senior high schools, since subjects are usually departmentalized, it is logical to have class newspapers or magazines reflect the different subject areas.

The same is true of foreign language publications. If these are

How Should A Teacher Teach?

I am sure this question has entered many teachers' minds, as well as many students minds. How can a teacher know when to stop bringing in personal opinions? An illustration of this is, if in a Social Studies class, or in an English class, a teacher should not determine the meaning behind an essay or a poem. The teacher should allow his or her students to form their own opinions, and then debate them. If the teacher disagrees with the students, then he should voice his own opinion, but go no farther. It is not fair, in a question of doubt for a teacher to force his own beliefs on a free thinking student. One of the basic goals of teaching is to make the student think. If any child is forced into someone else's thinking he will never try to think for himself — But allow everyone else to think for him.

If a teacher becomes angry when his student questions what he says, he is defeating the whole purpose

—Composition by Lisa Karlin

class efforts, start with the premise that each child can make some contribution. In this area, perhaps, the simplest is a list of translations of sayings. Each child who has contributed nothing else can take a statement and put it into the foreign tongue (or, incidentally, vice versa). These have real significance. We hear such phrases as "Caveat emptor" often. Shouldn't our young people be able to interpret this in English? Sketches, caricatures and anecdotes are all possibilities which will enrich the final product. In preparing any class publication you may assign children called class writers to assist the others, in preparation of the material. This makes it easier for everyone to contribute.

Special publications in subjects such as mathematics are possibilities, as well, and equally valuable. Their values lie primarily in their use as motivational devices, and then in their serving as source material for use with subsequent classes. Social studies lends itself to the preparation of a news sheet. One novel approach which is effective is to have the paper written as if the children lived in another time. This may be the future or the past—the 25th century or the 15th. As in the preparation of any paper, research should be an important part of it—for, as far as possible, all material in print should be accurate.

DUPLICATING OR PRINTING

These class newspapers or magazines should be duplicated within the school, by rexograph or mimeograph. Enough copies should be made to distribute one to each child who has been involved, and class sets should be prepared for use with future classes.

The production of the school literary magazine and yearbook should be by professional means. If the school has a printing shop which can produce copy which is up to professional standards, this will cut expenses considerably. If not, there are many professional printers who will bid for the contract. It is often possible to save money by preparing the magazine or yearbook for publication early in the year. Because these printers do the bulk of their work late in the spring, their prices are often less when they are less

YO NO QUIERO JUGUETES

Mi querido Santa Claus,

No es para mi que te pido.
Te pido por mi amiguita,
Una ninita extranjera
Que no hace mucho llego.

Me dice que no cree en nada
Me cuerta que alla en su tierra
Santa Claus no los visita
Que ella no cree en Santa Claus.

Dice que alla en su pais
Solo van los Reyes Magos
Y acostumbran visitar
Las casas adineradas.

No la olvides Santa Claus
Has que se restaure su fe
Ella quiere una muneca, un piano,
Una bicicleta, y unas tacitas de te.

Para mi no traigas nada,
No te preocupes por mi.
Me scntire muy contenta
Si mi amiguita es feliz.

Maria Gonzalez
8-301

I DON'T WANT ANY TOYS

My Dearest Santa Claus,

I am not asking anything for myself
I am asking for my friend,
A foreign girl
That not too long ago arrived.

She tells me that she doesn't believe in
anything.
She tells me that in her country
Santa Claus doesn't visit,
That she doesn't believe in Santa Claus.

She tells me that in her country
Only the Three Wise Men visit
And they are only accustomed
To stop at the houses of the rich.

Don't forget her, Santa Claus,
Let her hope be renewed.
She wants a doll, a piano, a bicycle,
And some cups for tea.

Don't bring me anything,
Don't worry about me.
I will feel very happy
If my friend is pleased.

Translation by the author.

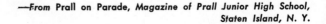

—From Prall on Parade, Magazine of Prall Junior High School,
Staten Island, N. Y.

busy. We suggest you shop around for the best prices, and make your own "deals."

The school newspaper, too, should be printed in the school, if at all possible, to cut down on expenses. If money is no object, it can, of course, be done by a professional print shop. We feel this publication should be distributed to every child in the school free of charge.

CHOOSING THE FACULTY ADVISOR
AND STUDENT STAFF

In regard to the newspaper, magazine or yearbook, the faculty advisor should have certain characteristics. He should be a volunteer, a person who is seeking an outlet for his own creativity, and one who will enjoy the task. He cannot be someone who is working on many projects, because he needs much time in order to do a good job. He must be the type of person, too, who will instill in the youngsters a desire to work and to cooperate. He should be someone who is knowledgeable, or willing to learn. In the case of the latter, there must be someone capable of training him. He must, above all, be a person who works well with others, because each of these ventures must represent the labors of many people.

To staff any of the publications, ask for volunteers and choose children who are motivated and interested. Try to select not only those who are very bright, but those who are seeking to become involved in the publication. We believe, too, that all of the children should be on the same level, and that there are no "editors," "reporters" and the like. Give every child an equal title, and make all of them feel important. We suggest the entire staff be trained in every task so that all can pitch in when a particular task needs to be done. Do not expect the children to be aware of what, specifically, is expected of them. Work with them, training them in all of the aspects of publishing.

In many schools, the literary magazine and the yearbook are combined into a single volume. This has proven effective on the elementary and junior high levels. You may use previous issues as

The Drug Addict
Interview and Analysis

by MARIE TINSLEY and ANGELA SARGEANT

This Halsey reporter recently interviewed a drug addict. We shall call her Sue Jones, a fictitious name for obvious reasons.

Sue is twenty years old and lives in Brooklyn. She attended the Bronx High School of Science. During those high school years Sue grew to have an uncontrollable complex. She felt that no one cared for her. Provoking and further complicating the problem was the death of both of Sue's parents. After that Sue went to live with an older sister.

Because of a growing defiance and hostile attitude Sue ran into many problems. Her average went from an "A" to a "B." Sue tried to pull herself up, but feeling as she did about other people made her stay back. At eighteen she graduated with an academic diploma. She had hoped to attend Michigan State College where she would have studied chemistry. Sue didn't make it. Shortly after graduation Sue got hooked on drugs. Her future was out of her hands.

Anxious to know more about the "how" and "why," this reporter asked Sue the following questions.

HOW DO YOU FEEL AFTER USING THIS DRUG? "Sometimes sick, sometimes good, sometimes I don't feel anything. It depends on the mood I'm in when I take it."

DOES TAKING DRUGS AFFECT YOUR FRIENDS AND FAMILY? "I don't live with my parents because they are dead. My sister is married and doesn't care and my brother is on the stuff too. My friends, you tell me. The only friend I have is myself. I hate phony people and everyone is phony. Sure I know people but I have no friends."

WHAT DO YOU EXPECT OF PEOPLE? "Just to love and help me. I never did anything to anyone. It's just that this dirty world won't give a person a chance to prove anything of themselves. And people just hate one another terribly."

DO YOU THINK I'M A PHONY? "No, you're just nosy. And people can be nosy also. All people are nosy and phony."

DO YOU WANT TO STOP TAKING DRUGS? "I don't know what I want to do. I don't think about it."

HAVE YOU ANY ADVICE TO OTHER PEOPLE? "Who am I to say anything? The world looks like a big ball of nothing to me. They didn't care about me because I was a tall, dark, nappy-headed Negro with a brain, so why should I care about them. I go to church on Sundays and I see a bunch of phony, sinning, so-called Christian people. As long as you are in the church, they smile. But when you get outside, they call you names. People are just phony, phony, phony."

HOW DO YOU ENVISION YOUR FUTURE? "What future? God knows, I've tried to help myself many times. I've tried to stop but I can't kick it. It's hard to."

Perhaps Sue Jones' main problem is self pity. Some of the unfairness she points up, such as racial prejudice, is genuine. But she isn't the only victim of it. Rather than trying to do something positive about it, such as going to a college other than her first choice and "making" it in life, she has succumbed and consequently is nowhere. Perhaps she is using this as an excuse for a weakness that is greater in her than in society.

The fact that Sue has no parents is unfortunate. Even more unfortunate is Sue's belief that no one cares for her. At this point one is inclined to ask: Has Sue given people the chance to befriend her? Are all people really as nosy and phony as she suggests? We think not. Give people a chance and you'll discover they'll do the same for you. Not all, but more than not. Sue's lack of friends intensifies her feelings of rejection. Being friendless, Sue's loneliness is even greater.

Not finding the understanding, support and companionship she needed from people, Sue looked elsewhere. She turned to drugs. Did she find those things there. No! She says she is still lonely and unhappy; she still doesn't have friends; she has no future to look forward to. By using drugs she is punishing herself even more. She builds herself up, just to be let down again. This increases her depression, which only makes her worse after believing so strongly in her dreams.

To conclude, Sue's answer is no answer. Her only salvation is to "kick" her habit, pull herself together, and keep the faith. Without faith, she'll never be anywhere.

—*Editorial from Halsey Herald, Newspaper of
Halsey Junior High School, Brooklyn, N. Y.*

guides. Encourage the staff to improve upon these. Make your publications as relevant as possible to the children's lives.

The theme of the literary magazine (and yearbook) should be suggested by the children. Since many young people are very involved in the problems of the world, they are often anxious to contribute ideas for the themes. Some which you may find useful are, "How can we work for a better world?" "Brotherhood," "Improving the lives of everyone in our community," "The feelings of the youth of today," "Love and hate," "Emotions," and of course, "Peace on earth, good will to all men."

CENSORSHIP

We feel that, in order to give your young people the greatest opportunities to express themselves, you establish certain guidelines at the beginning of the year and then censor as little as possible. We believe the publications should reflect the educational process so that all language used must be in good taste. But we believe very strongly that young people should be allowed to discuss, in print, things about which they feel strongly. As adults, we should not feel threatened by these young voices. They need a forum to give their opinions and to hear the voices of other young people. Editorials, feature stories, and "Letters to the Editor" can be vital and interesting—if the boys and girls can write about topics in which they are really involved. If the pupils feel their work will be censored, they lose interest and their products reflect their disinterest. Censorship is, at best, a necessary evil. At its worst, it can stifle initiative and creativity.

The editorial reproduced on page 160 was removed from a school newspaper. Written by an eighth grader, it was interpreted as an attack on a teacher. It is our feeling that the material could have been printed and discussed in classes, with good results. By its removal, the writer was antagonized and made unhappy.

We are not advocating relinquishing our roles as adults, educators, and guides. We are asking that we refrain from being rigid or inflexible—but that we move with the tides and with the times. Why should it be considered a threat for children to discuss dress

TO A HOPELESS WORLD

My soul is scorched;
It is beginning to crumble!
Like a rat in a maze,
I am bewildered - lost.
Somewhere
Near the other side of Time,
I'll find a hole in the wall,
And I'll be able to wriggle through.
Oh, no,
It's not myself I pity;
I'll find my answers.
For I know if they're not in Today,
They are waiting in Tomorrow.
But what about you?
You can't always hide behind your Image.
Someday someone will strip you,
And you will have to stand
Naked.
Those little bugs that we call Truth,
They will feast on your flesh,
And I will cry.
But can't you see - I'm crying today,
For I know what awaits and. . . . .
I'm afraid!

Lisa Karlin

*—From Atheneum, Magazine of Susan E. Wagner High School,
Staten Island, N. Y.*

or hair styles? Yet many advisors and administrators refuse to permit such discussions, in print. If soul searching is necessary, please do so. Try to make your censorship minimal—and the cooperation of the children will probably be maximal, as a result.

SERVANT OF TIME

Hurry! Keep busy!
Occupy your hands;
Never dare stop moving.
Dizzy brain churn endlessly!
   Wind will whisper melodiously;
   Night will hush the sea;
   Mist will rise in silver curls
   And twine around the trees.
All - all this is lost to your eyes,
Blind and willing Slave of Time,
Filling each day of precious life

With problems sprung anew.
You think your hours have been put
To good and worthy cause
While pictures that can live but once,
Unnoticed slip away.
   The dying rays that pierce the dusk,
   You take no pause to see.
   You stumble blindly through each task;
   How dead your soul must be!
   For living lies not in hours of labor,
   But in one crowning moment FREE!

Amy Rice

—From Atheneum, Magazine of Susan E. Wagner High School,
Staten Island, N. Y.

Editorial

The assembly is supposed to be a place where besides learning about school policy, students can express certain feelings, and demonstrate their abilities to their peers, whether they be extremely bright, good athletes or talented in arts. In all fairness, some assembly programs have been enjoyable. The modern dance group's recital was very well received; after all, what's to be wrong with pretty girls displaying their talents tastefully?

Another assembly program which students enjoyed was the performance by Mr. McCarthy's Senior Band. The reason students liked the assembly was that the band played many popular tunes. The orchestra also performed at the assembly yet the students did not appreciate this as much for the simple reason that an orchestra performs works which are classical, baroque or romantic in nature. But every program should be appealing to its audience. In an era of "everything power", one wonders why some of the individuals, or groups who demand a greater degree of involvement in their local school don't volunteer their talents to improve the situation.

Logically, this talent should originate from the student body. We consider it frankly illogical that adults plan what should be adolescent entertainment. Miss Valerie Stratton is indeed a lovely person and a gifted teacher, but planning an exciting or memorable period requires help. The remedy to the problem is to organize an assembly advisory council. This group should consist of any interested and imaginative G.O. member who believes he can contribute worthwhile suggestions.

This could be achieved by testing 10 or more suggestions for the assembly for one month, and circulating the list to all the home-rooms to have the students vote on those they would like to see. So, let's go, gang; get up off your seat and become involved in vitalizing this aspect of school life.

If we don't start calling the assembly plays, those kindly old, well meaning (but frequently over 30) people will just have to continue trying to do their best.

—Editorial from Wagner World, Susan E. Wagner High School,
Staten Island, N. Y.

TRAINING STUDENTS IN PREPARING PUBLICATIONS

Sales of a publication will be determined to a large extent by the number of boys and girls whose work appears therein. The school literary magazine and yearbook should not be the province of a small group of youngsters whose writing talents are quite evident. They should, instead, reflect the work of the entire school.

This can be accomplished in a number of ways. Language arts teachers can assign topics, with the assurance to the boys and girls that their work will be considered for publication. Poetry, compositions, short stories, and plays would fall into this subject area. In social studies, problems in regard to community and current events might be written about. Each teacher in the school should be encouraged to submit the best work done in his classes to the editorial staff, regardless of subject area.

In a yearbook, it is possible to have a section devoted to paragraphs about each class, composed by the entire group. These might refer to exciting things the class had done or learned. In this way each class makes a significant contribution. It is up to the language arts teachers to make them readable and interesting.

After the written material has been selected, it may be turned over to the art department, for illustration, and the students, having read some of the subject matter, will be able to create drawings, paintings, and designs which are pertinent. The work selected should be printed on the same page, or the page facing the work they illustrate. The cover, particularly, should be relative to the theme of the book.

All work to be published, be it literary or art, should be selected by the staff of the magazine or yearbook, and should reflect the best the school has to offer.

The photographs which are used should be of high quality, whether taken by professional photographers or students. Candid photos and action shots are particularly effective, but should never look posed. These may be taken by pupils. The group photos of classes, teams and clubs are more often taken by professionals. These should be taken against a simple background, so that the faces of the students are clearly visible. If they are not, the photograph should not be used, for if the boys and girls are not easily recognizable, the pictures lose their value.

The material which has been selected to appear in the publication is sent to the printer, and he returns it in the form of rough galley proofs. The editorial staff reads these carefully, and then uses them to make a dummy which is used in the paste-up.

The various articles, stories, poems and pieces of art work are then cut apart and placed on pages. This is called the lay-out. It is the task of those doing the lay-outs to provide attractive arrangements of printed material and white space on each page. Pages which face each other should balance, but each page should be well arranged within itself. After this is done, the materials are pasted on the pages, and the dummy is made. This consists of the complete book or magazine, with each page pasted up as it is desired in print, placed in the dummy. A rough lay-out and dummy may be made, to be followed by a final or master dummy. This must be perfect, because it will be photographed, for reproduction in the yearbook or magazine.

Each of the steps outlined above should be done by pupils trained in this type of work. Many times the printer can be of great help, particularly if the faculty advisor is a relative novice, in training the students.

Preparing a magazine or yearbook for publication involves a great deal of hard work, but it is very rewarding and can be a memorable experience for the youngsters.

PUBLISHING A NEWSPAPER

A newspaper poses many different problems. It should contain school news, features, interviews, cartoons, human interest stories, puzzles, and "Inquiring Photographer," "Letters to the Editor," reviews of movies, records and books, and material of interest to the boys and girls. One feature which was thoroughly enjoyed was "Meet Our New Teachers." Another was a photograph of a baby, with the caption "Guess Who I Am." The photographs used were usually those of teachers, who were beautiful babies! Sports coverage is important in any newspaper, and articles such as "Know Your Team" prove exciting to the students.

Above all, the newspaper should contain news of events within the school and community, of the doings of the Student Government, of trips taken by various classes, of guests who have visited, of dances and other social events. It should be *the* means of communication within the school. Consider a "Lonely Hearts" column, or a "Want Ads" section, too. It is possible to have the newspaper mimeographed, if funds for its printing are not avail-

by Joan Zelman

"The Loves of Isadora" is the tragic story of the dancer Isdora Duncan, a free and wild individual. Vanessa Redgrave, as Isadora, radiates the spirit that possessed her, and with the aid of expressive camera work and superb fellow actors,   creates   what in many ways maybe the best movie of the year.

As you ride along through the real America, with fitting folk and rock music surrounding you, an absurd sort of humor, the dominent tone of **Easy Rider**, manifests itself. It goes on to reveal its exceptional style by a gradual, but definite turning point in its mood, so that you leave the theatre disturbed and thinking about America-the-beautiful and the hateful. For face value, a young audience could identify only, but probing deeper into the basic theme one finds ideas that all can relate to and learn from.

Peter Fonda, Dennis Hopper (also director) and Jack Nicholson as leads, succeeded in making "ugly" items like motorcyclists and hippies seem real and beautiful and in making America the most real, beautiful, yet violent of all lands.

Movie Review   by Lisa Karlin

Alice's Restaurant is the movie based on the song (by Arlo Guthrie) with the same name. Though the movie takes the theme of the song, it is extended into a sensitive account of hippies and the people who affect them.

The character development is excellent, and the action is fast moving. Though the overall theme is humorous there are many scenes with horrifying but realistic pictures of life and death. The acting is good with Arlo playing himself quite creditably. This movie appeals mostly to a young audience which can easily identify with it.

Record Review

Blood, Sweat and Tears is the second album by this group. The first album had the talent of Al Kooper mixed with the group itself, but this recording portrays Blood, Sweat, and Tears alone. The album is a union of good jazz and rock, united to produce an exceptional combination. Although we enjoyed the first album more, the later one seems to have a wider circle of fans. The excellent interpretation of Lauro Nyro's, "And When I Die" plus their own "Sometimes In Winter" enhance this recording immensely. The hit number "Spinning Wheel" also helps to make this album as good as it is. We think it should be an enjoyable experience for any rock listener.

—Excerpt from Wagner World, *Susan E. Wagner High School, Staten Island, N. Y.*

able. However, the methods of financing are applicable to both newspapers and magazines.

The same type of staff is needed for the newspaper as was outlined above for the magazine. Because it comes out more frequently, having more youngsters write for it may help to meet the deadlines. As we said before, the more children involved, the more interest, and the better the sales.

Fund Raising

There are a number of sources for funds for the school publications: the dues paid by the students each year toward their Student Government should, in part, be used for the newspaper and the magazine. However, it's always necessary to augment this with advertising. It has been found that advertisers in school publications should be approached early in the year. Many schools use this means of fund-raising, and if yours is one of the first, you may be more fortunate than if you wait until the middle of the year. Some of the possible advertisers include the shops in your neighborhood, banks, insurance firms, parents owning businesses, unions, firms with which the school does business, private schools in your area, such as music schools, and schools for specialized work such as beauty culture, which seek to attract graduates.

Your rates should be similar to those charged by other schools in your area. To obtain ads, it is wise to have individual students sell advertising, or to use a committee of students, who visit potential advertisers. Make sure they are properly dressed and groomed, and know their subject. You may wish to canvas the area by mail, as well, but this is not as successful as the personal approach. We have found that one of our art teachers devised a technique which was eminently successful. She made each advertisement unique by adding a cartoon or design to it. The advertisers were simply delighted, and never failed to renew their ads from year to year. The renewal of ads is a most important source of revenue, and these advertisers should be contacted as soon as the advertising campaign is undertaken. It is possible to contact them by telephone or mail, if personal visits are difficult to arrange.

Magazine boosters may be sold to parents, friends and to organizations. Classes may be encouraged to purchase advertising space, and many of the class ads have proven to be delightful.

The yearbook is financed, quite often, fully or in part by the class dues, which the graduating class pays each year. Here, too, booster ads and class advertisements may be sold to help defray costs.

In order to raise the large amount of money often needed to cover expenses, we have found that a contest can be used to exite the children, and to motivate them. We have offered prizes to the three pupils selling the most advertisements, and the class raising the most money was taken on a trip. Then the number of prizes was raised to six. We used transistor radios for the five runner-ups, and a camera for the best salesman. We allowed the top class to select the place for the trip themselves, which really delighted them.

MAKING THE PUBLICATIONS INTERESTING
TO THE CHILDREN AND TO THE ENTIRE COMMUNITY

1) Choose a good name, a name which is attention getting. One of the most unusual we have heard is "Zenger's Press." Try to avoid the trite, and the prosaic such as "Central News." We were very enthused by the name "Indecision" which was used, temporarily, by one school newspaper, until it became "The Communicator."

2) Have the newspaper and magazine reflect the ideas and views of the young people in the school, rather than the faculty advisors, or the administration. Ask the staff to suggest subjects for articles, and for art work. Have them choose the theme. Have meetings of the staffs at times when the boys and girls can easily attend. In short, get the students interested and involved and then allow them to take it from there.

3) Don't be afraid of controversy. If academic freedom is fostered, subject always to the rules of good taste, the publications will really become vehicles for the expression of public opinion. Try to present all the sides of any issue, rather than merely one or two. Even ideas which have been around for many years, such

—Cover from Prall on Parade, Magazine of Prall Junior High School,
Staten Island, N. Y.

as the "18 year old vote," are capable of stirring up the youngsters. Or perhaps they would react to "A Woman for President of the U.S.A." Topics such as these are excellent as foci, around which youngsters can consolidate their opinions.

4) Hold contests. These are excellent ways of getting students involved. The contests may be profound—such as "Prepare a

Time Capsule, to represent present day civilization. What would you put into it?" Or, the more lighthearted, "How can we decorate the school for Halloween?" Naming contests are fun, as puzzles are. The old device, "How many words can you find in _____," (Use the name of your school) is good. Cartoons can be used, with blanks left for the boys and girls to fill in the speech balloons.

5) *Profiles*—In-depth, thorough interviews with teachers or pupils are interest-provoking. Choose colorful personalities, who will make amusing or arresting statements. The fact that Mr. Jones watches football games on Sunday afternoon will not prove nearly as interesting as the fact that he had worked his way through college as a store detective in a huge department store. "Meet Your New Teachers and Supervisors" is a favorite column of many boys and girls.

6) If anyone connected with the school has done something of general interest, it should be written up. Many of our young people have traveled far and wide, and have fascinating stories to tell. Why not print them in either the newspaper or the magazine? One boy had spent the summer working on his father's fishing boat. His stories made a fascinating article.

7) Have a column called, "It's Your Opinion." Then ask a question of many pupils, and print the results. The question may refer to current events, to social problems, or to philosophical subjects. Have the youngsters determine the questions, and prepare articles using the responses.

8) Discuss problems which relate to the particular age group which is represented. You may wish to use the following format: Parent and child have a difference of opinion. Have the parent state his side, then have the young person give his views. Then have a guidance counselor, or a psychologist try to work out a compromise or settlement between the two.

9) Articles and columns in regard to clothing and grooming are of interest to many young people. These may be made even more relevant if they are in the form of questions and answers. If few questions are forthcoming, these may be composed by the author of the column.

10) Be sure there is a diversity of material in either the maga-

zine or the newspaper so that there is something to interest every reader. Remember, too, that parents will read the publications put out by the children. If you wish to, you may ask them for comments and for opinions—and give them the space in which they may reply.

11) Filler is used in every newspaper and magazine. Why not ours? Short anecdotes, funny stories or interesting facts have been used very successfully. For example, one teacher we know mentioned Noah's Ark and asked the children who had heard of it. One boy raised his hand.

"Where did you hear of it?" asked the teacher.

"Oh," replied the child, "I saw it, I saw the first one. The original!"

"You saw it! Where?"

"In the movies!"

Invite the boys and girls to contribute even short, short stories. Some are too good to miss.

12) Include news of community events which are relevant to the lives of the children. Dances, shows, exhibits, family parties may all be mentioned. It is a good idea, every so often, to call attention to the recreational facilities in the area, or easily reached by car or public transportation. Ice skating, swimming, football games, or tennis might, for example, be mentioned.

Student publications serve many purposes within the school and community. They are the outlet for creative expression—the opportunity for the young people to speak out, to give voice to their feelings, their beliefs, their values.

The literary magazine, the yearbook and the newspaper all represent the school and its students. They are the tangible statement—"this is what we are; these words, these pages represent us." The publications of each school are unique, and well they should be—for they are the result of the work of many individuals. They give these individuals, however, opportunities to work together, planning, preparing and publishing. The roles of the faculty should be as guides, rather than as contributors.

It is well for the students to remember that the function of any printed page is to communicate. Through the school publications

*—Advertisement from Prall on Parade, Magazine of
Prall Junior High School, Staten Island, N. Y.*

their voices are heard by their parents, friends, and members of the community. It is important, therefore, that they reflect a true picture of the school and its pupils, its educational activities, its student activities program; in short a record of the life of the school.

Holding an   **10**

"Event-of-the-Year"

Each school needs one huge event held yearly; one major effort involving every department, and hopefully every single child. For the same reasons that the productions mentioned in Chapter 8 are necessary, this event is needed. It should create excitement throughout the school—for weeks in advance. It may take the form of a Country Fair, or a Field Day, an Open House, or a Trip Around the World. Whatever form it takes, it should be the talk of the school, the spark which kindles the imagination of the children and faculty alike, and it should involve as much of the work of the school and curriculum as possible. This should not be a show solely for the sake of entertainment, but an exhibition and activity of value primarily to the children. They should look forward to it, plan for it, work on it—and above all, be exhilarated by it.

We are going to describe such an event to you in detail. It is one with which one of the authors has been closely associated for five years, and one which has always proved to be worth the hours upon hours of work, and the blood, sweat and tears which have gone into it. The formal names of our event are "Our Winter Festival of Learning" or "Prall Parades for Parents"— and it truly is, in The Anning S. Prall School, the Event-of-the-Year.

THE WINTER FESTIVAL

The Winter Festival, as it is always referred to by children and teachers, was the creation of the principal, Mr. Norman H. Harris. As a result of visits to the New York World's Fair of 1964 and 1965, he suggested we have our own "World's Fair" right in the school. Every department was to be represented, and most important, as many pupils as possible were to be included.

It was decided to hold the program in the evening, and to invite parents and members of the community. They were to be shown the regular work the students were doing—although it is true that, as time goes on, this is elaborated upon because the children try harder and harder to outdo the festival of the previous year.

To launch the program, department chairmen and key personnel were invited to a luncheon meeting in the principal's office. The idea was bandied about, various suggestions were made, and the chairmen took the ideas back to their teachers. Department meetings were held, and further discussion took place. Then the teachers went to work on the program with their students. No one was told what to do—nor have they ever been, in the five years that we have held the festivals. All the exhibits and performances came from either the teachers or the pupils. The results the first year, and every subsequent year, were far beyond our expectations. As chairman of the event for four of the five years, I can truthfully say there are always surprises, always something to become really excited about, and always the glow of happiness and delight on the children's faces.

To continue with our description of the procedures we used: a flyer was sent out to describe the program and to determine how many tickets each pupil wanted. As requests kept coming in the number increased quickly. We had originally printed six hundred, then another six hundred, and still another—all the way up to almost two thousand. Our print shop came to the rescue, as usual. The tickets were distributed, and the children were given special passes to enter the building, known as Participant Passes.

A second luncheon meeting was held just before the program to complete work on the myriad details. We find this is very pleasant, but not a necessity. There are always some bits or pieces which have to be done at the last moment, but for the most part the festival runs smoothly now. The adage "Experience is the best teacher" is so true!

ACTIVITIES

To enable our visitors to see as much as possible of our work, we divided the program into three parts. The first part consisted of band and chorus performances in the auditorium. Slides created by students of the art classes were shown while the chorus and the band performed. This proved to be very exciting. The second part was an exhibition, held in the gymnasium, of the athletic skills and the folk dancing taught in the health education classes. The third part, a "World's Fair of Academic Subjects," was set up in the cafeteria.

In addition to these major areas, there were other exhibits. The woodworking and metalworking shops were kept open, with interesting displays from all of the industrial arts classes. (The shops are conveniently located near the auditorium.) In the main lobby, on one side, a travel booth, with foreign language students singing folk songs and strumming guitars was a big attraction. The students were colorfully dressed in charming costumes. On the other side of the lobby, emulating the artists of the West Bank, several of our talented boys and girls were seated at their easels, making pictures for the visitors. Other art work decorated the walls and beautified the halls.

That first year more than 150 youngsters performed in the orchestra and chorus. The health education department presented a wonderful opportunity for those pupils who do not excel in academic pursuits to show their physical prowess—and show it they did! The broadjumping events had the entire audience holding its breath.

And again, we want to emphasize the fact that no child whose health record or whose doctor has forbidden such activities, was participating. Such children were encouraged to take part in some other part of the festival, which would not be detrimental to their health or well-being.

In the cafeteria the floor area was divided to give all the other departments space for their exhibits. The social studies classes had a showing which included slides, lecture material, and, finally, audience participation, in "Vote for Your Favorite President." Foreign language students put on a puppet show—written, produced and directed, and acted by the children, themselves. The science department had various exhibits such as the dissection of a fetal pig (lifeless, of course) being done by eighth grade students, who explained each step to interested spectators. The mathematics pupils had a fascinating display involving measurements. Everyone crowded around the Child Care Center, where toys the students had made were on display. "The Birth of a Magazine," was part of the exhibit of the language arts department. Other classes wrote and printed wonderful books for children. The fore-

—Official Photograph, Board of Education, City of New York

DISSECTION DEMONSTRATION

Winter Festival guests are most interested in this type of biological exploration.

going in the briefest of summaries of the work shown that first year—exhibits, which showed originality, exhibited with great pride.

To move the crowds efficiently, tickets were printed in three colors. This device divided the guests into three groups, of approximately six hundred each. Holders of the red tickets, went to the auditorium first; then they went to the gymnasium, and finally to the cafeteria. Each aspect took about forty-five minutes. Holders of the green tickets visited the cafeteria first, then the auditorium next, and then the gymnasium. Yellow tickets admitted their holders to the gymnasium first, then to the cafeteria, and to the auditorium last. The plan was eminently successful, and we are still using it. Three performances are given by the pupils participating in the auditorium, and three by those in the gymnasium. To involve more children, it is possible to have a different group of children perform each time, or possibly have two groups; one performing once, and the other twice. For, as we must stress, we involve as many of the pupils as we possibly can.

THE IMPORTANCE OF PLANNING

We knew we had a "hit" when we discovered the pupils had a black market in tickets; they were being sold for prices up to twenty-five cents each on the day of that first festival.

But what is a party without refreshments? The home economics pupils, guided by their teachers, made and served apple pancakes and cider in the cafeteria. (The prevalence of apples was because they had been donated—as had the cider.) Cafeteria personnel were employed to assist with the kitchen equipment.

In setting up a similar program, many factors must be considered. The program requires time for planning, and should be announced early in the school year. Teachers are then able to select for exhibition the best work done in their classes as the term progresses. The Winter Festival should not conflict with other school performances, such as the Science Fair or dramatic or musical programs.

We have never used the Festival for fund raising, and in fact we have had to spend money for some small purchases. However, in recent years we have been selling gifts, and other small items in our "Boutique,"—all handcrafted by the children. In this way, the Festival has been able to become self-sustaining.

Some of the newer developments have been tremendously exciting. We have had English teachers set up "Little Theatres," and one performance of "Sorry, Wrong Number," was so outstanding that, three years after its production, we are still hearing comments about it from members of the community. Another Language Arts class became interested in ghosts, and their production involved discussion, a play and audience participation. Other classes did dramas of their own composition, and one group even prepared a newspaper. We've had a "Las Vegas Night," to

—Official Photograph, Board of Education, City of New York

FUN WITH GEOMETRY

Games add interest and enjoyment of the curriculum, as seen at Prall's Winter Festival.

show the odds involved in betting, called by the proper name, Permutations and Combinations. Experiments galore were performed by the science students involving the laws of physics, the scientific method and countless others.

There was a Hav-a-Java Coffee Shop, in which the waiters and waitresses were in costume. One outstanding attraction was the Japanese tea ceremony performed by a social studies class. An exhibition of Karate attracted the attention of everyone. One year we had an exhibit done by ceramics classes which consisted of changing the shapes of bottles. These were beautiful enough to have been placed in any museum. Masks, mobiles and montages are always in evidence. We try to choose a particularly effective display for the main entrance, and on one occasion had huge paper flowers, which the girls in the home economics classes had made. These were part of a flower stand, where they were sold at one dollar a flower, and were all gone by the end of the first hour. Fortunately above the stand had been written, in smaller flowers, the words, "Welcome to Prall." These are only a few examples. There are hundreds more.

SO MANY BENEFITS!

When the idea of holding that first Winter Festival was brought up, there were moans and groans, but as the date neared, the excitement grew. The school became alive with pupils working, and one could see and feel their enthusiasm, which indeed was contagious. The children were so involved, so proud and so anxious, all at the same time!

The same is true today, although now the Festival is a tradition of the school. Many of the faculty and all of the children look forward to it. As one teacher told Mr. Harris, after that first one, "I didn't like the idea at first, but, when the kids caught fire, so did I. For instance, I never dreamed I could do committee work with some of these boys; but my slowest classes got so enthusiastic about suggesting different projects we could do that I found them doing committee work on their own."

There is no question but that the teachers of the music and

health education departments must contribute a great deal of their time and effort if the Festival is to succeed, for they carry the burden of preparing two of the three performances given. However, they use the Festival for motivation, and have always come through with really fabulous entertainments. The musical finale is usually a truly outstanding piece of music, performed by many, many children—with such seriousness and dedication that there is no possibility of mistaking their involvement and their sincerity. And in this group there are often children who have been discipline problems. In fact, during the Festival there is so much action, so much going on that even the truants come to school. I recall one boy who had been in school a total of 28 days before the Festival, but who came in to arrange the seating in the gymnasium.

Why Does the Festival Take Place in Winter?

One of Mr. Harris' purposes in selecting winter, and even in naming this the Winter Festival, was because this season is traditionally a sleepy time, with doldrums setting in, and a certain lethargic feeling prevailing. But not now! Everyone is just too busy planning and executing. Many teachers start to consult with their classes in October or November, but often the real work is done during those weeks after we return from Christmas vacation: we have always had the Festival the last week in January or the first week in February. It has always been successful, and this in spite of the fact that we have been caught up in the middle of snowstorms. People manage to get to the school, and once inside, it teems with activity.

One of the main problems in setting up has been the rapid cleaning of the cafeteria, but our custodial staff has always been very helpful, and our supervisors not above using a mop themselves. After the last lunch period, the floors are done, and the tables placed so that each area is set aside for the various displays. Space has been requested beforehand, so that the division may be planned, somewhat, in advance. Then, at about two o'clock, the children are permitted to come down and set up their exhibits. Chaos reigns! Anyone who cannot stand disorder has to stay away.

—Official Photograph, Board of Education, City of New York

DEMONSTRATION OF POTTERY-MAKING

The Honorable Isaiah Robinson, Jr., New York City Board of Education member, and Mr. Norman H. Harris, principal of Prall Junior High School, view young creators at work at the Winter Festival.

But by three, at dismissal time, most of the work is done, and at four the doors are locked, and everyone sent home for a rest and dinner. Then at six thirty the doors are opened to participants, and at 6:45 to guests. The first performance starts at 7:00 and ends at 7:45. The second starts at 8:00 and ends at 8:45, and the last at 9:00, ending at 9:45. Doors close by 10:15, and everyone goes home exhausted, but happy.

This project is a device which can be used in any school to help eliminate mid-winter doldrums, and help to earn community goodwill. Most of all, it can help to improve the self-image of all of the children in the school. For the sensitive, self-effacing child, it can be the birth of self-confidence, and the discovery of hidden gifts. For the child who tends to be anti-social, it can be a medium for working with his peers on wholesome activities, rather than on destructive ones. For the hyperactive child, it can be a channel for the constructive release of much energy that might otherwise tend to make him troublesome.

A festival is synonymous with happiness. One of our motives in our "Winter Festival of Learning," was to unite the efforts of all the pupils and teachers to attain pleasure through learning. In addition to this success, we have given our pupils an opportunity to shine, for every class is asked to contribute something. Of course many children contribute in more than one subject area, but if each class is in at least one, a great many children are involved.

Photographing the Winter Festival is always a joy, for there are so many interesting and amusing shots to be taken. We make sure that these are printed and placed on exhibit in the main lobby of the school, for all of the children to see. We try, too, to have pictures taken of visitors as well as students, of observers as well as participants. (If the Photography Club is able to do so, you may wish to present copies of the pictures of the guests to them. This may be done through the children in the school to whom they are related.)

Articles and photographs in the school newspaper, in preparation for, and after the Winter Festival, are of value, we have found. The human interest approach is a good one. We have boys and girls acting as reporters, ferreting out information, interviewing guests as well as participants.

REACTION OF THE COMMUNITY

We have always enjoyed the most favorable of reviews from our parents, and guests. As the fame of the Festival has grown, so has the attendance. One year it was over four thousand, but this, we found, was too many for us to accommodate comfortably.

For several years we have been interviewed on the radio and had guests from miles and miles away, as a result. Members of the School Board are honored guests, and in recent years we have had other prominent people attend. Each year brings something different, something unexpected. And each year, too, there is a human interest story. Once, for example, a play was being performed, and one of the boys who had been walking the halls advertising the play in his costume, suddenly had an epileptic seizure. Fortunately it was a mild one; he recovered quickly, and insisted upon performing. How could we refuse? So everyone held his breath, and all went well. No one in the audience had any idea of the events preceding the performance. At another time, one of the girls who was to sing a solo was told by her physician she could not strain her voice. She did not reveal this to her teacher, but went on—and in the midst of her song her voice gave out. She excused herself, giving the reason and asked that she be permitted to start again, and this time she sang the song perfectly. There wasn't a dry eye in the audience.

Since the success of any endeavor of this sort is often measured by the number of guests who attend, the publicity given the event can be of great importance. In Chapter 10 we have outlined a number of methods which will apply to an affair of this kind, as well.

SHARING RESPONSIBILITY
AND DEVELOPING ENTHUSIASM

In order to avoid giving any one individual too much work to do, we suggest that you share responsibility, again in much the same way that is outlined in Chapter 10. We have found that when each department head or supervisor is responsible for his or her teachers, asks for progress reports, and in advance views the contributions being made by his teachers' classes, things go relatively smoothly. One person is needed to correlate the entire project, however, because we have found that an overall coordinator is a definite necessity. Equally necessary is motivation, and it is hoped that the Festival itself will supply that. If the teachers are enthusiastic, their classes will be; if they appear burdened or uninvolved, their boys and girls will react in the same manner. It is the task of the chairman, and of the supervisors to suggest ideas, to help to implement plans, and if any exhibits, plays or other features are unsuitable, to think of the means to remedy them— so that they become valuable contributions. Creative supervision is devoutly to be desired. There is no reason why previous successes cannot be repeated, for it is virtually impossible for every visitor to see everything, and furthermore viewings are a year apart.

We would like to invite any reader to attend the Festival. It would be our pleasure to send you tickets of admission—and traveling instructions. Please address your request to Mr. Norman H. Harris, Principal, Prall J.H.S., 11 Clove Lake Place, Staten Island, New York 10310. We promise you an evening you will thoroughly enjoy.

OTHER TYPES OF EXCITING EVENTS

The same principles govern any events of this nature as those we have suggested for the Winter Festival, be it a Country Fair or a Field Day, an Open House or a Trip Around the World. These include:

> Preplanning.
> Involving as many children as possible.
> Making the best possible use of all facilities.
> Selecting activities which the children will enjoy.
> Sharing responsibility.
> Informing the public of the event, and inviting
>   them to participate.

One elementary school has a highly successful Field Day held annually in the spring. The boys and girls march to a nearby park, where there are formal ceremonies opening the Field Day. Games and races, dances and songs follow. Then they are treated to a delicious picnic or barbeque lunch prepared by the Parent-Teacher Organization, and more activities follow. At two-thirty the entire group is taken back to the school by bus because everyone is deliciously exhausted. Before they leave the park prizes are awarded to the winners of the games and contests. The children

MAYPOLES AND CHILDREN GO HAND-IN-HAND

Happiness and gaiety are in evidence as boys and girls enjoy their dancing near beautifully decorated Maypoles.

look forward to this event for weeks before. An alternate date is chosen, in case of rain. Parents and members of the community are always invited, by letters written by the children, to take part.

There are events which require less preparation, such as an Open House, but even this should have many activities to show the parents. Demonstration lessons, some given by the girls and boys, should be prepared, and intriguing assembly programs planned.

A Country Fair could be run in a manner combining some of the activities of the Festival and the Field Day. Games, booths, contests and races would be featured. Food might be distributed, or sold at booths. There should be some events to liven things up —for example, possibly a Sadie Hawkins Dance (at which the girls ask the boys to dance) . The youngsters may be encouraged to wear Li'l Abner or Sadie Hawkins costumes, if they wish. The accent would be on country music, and the decor should match.

For a Trip Around the World, each classroom may be converted into something pertaining to a different nation. For example, some rooms might be museums, with collections of materials, photographs, paintings or drawings, handiwork, and natural resources. Another might be a restaurant, a third a sidewalk cafe. If a nation has produced a number of famous artists, and great art, the classroom might be a gallery and might feature reproductions of these works. Still another room might have costumes, or music, flags or furniture. If a nation has a famous landmark, this should be prominently displayed: for example, the leaning Tower of Pisa, the Eiffel Tower, or Big Ben and the Houses of Parliament. Have the children do as much research as necessary for them to be able to discuss "their land" fluently. They might even learn to greet visitors in the tongue spoken by the inhabitants. Expanding upon this theme is fun, and educational as well, and the resulting event can be quite thrilling.

Invite guests to any and all of these activities, for, as the children learn, they will also communicate their knowledge.

To have a truly effective program, it is almost axiomatic that the school must reach out and bring the parents and members of the community, into its confines. People should be able to see what their children, or their nieces and nephews or their neighbors' children are doing during the hours they are in school. If they know, they are more inclined to support the program, less inclined to criticize it unfavorably. By holding events such as those outlined, they can partake of the school program, and, at the same time enjoy themselves.

This is one of the purposes of the "Event of the Year," but it is not the most important one, for it is the effect this event has on the children which really counts. If they look forward to it, talk about it, participate in it and really enjoy it, then it has been successful. Special programs should be truly special—and especially the "Event-of-the-Year."

Encouraging Your Teachers and Students to Vigorously Support the Student Activities Program

11

No program in a school can be successful if its teachers and its parent groups are not actively involved in it. In this chapter we shall discuss the role of the teachers which is critical, for they are the most important contact the child has with the school. Any child's opinion of his school is derived in large measure from his reactions to his teachers. If they are enthused about anything, the chances are the child will be too. The opposite is also true—if the teacher is apathetic, then his pupils will probably behave in much the same manner. It then is essential that the teachers believe in, and "sell" the student activities program, if it is to succeed.

How can we enlist the active support of the teachers, and what shall they do to encourage the support of the children?

STAFFING THE STUDENT ACTIVITIES PROGRAM

By having your teachers staff the student activities program, whenever possible, you accomplish many goals concurrently. You encourage the good will of the teachers by hiring them, and paying them for their time. For many of the young people in the profession, who must take on second jobs because their salaries are insufficient to fulfill their needs, working in the school on extracurricular projects is heaven-sent. They save time traveling, and are using the skills they have developed—rather than doing other, unprofessional tasks. You improve the quality of the teaching, during the day as well, for the teacher is less tired, and less apt to "take it easy" in his class. Furthermore, he is anxious to please the administration.

The children benefit from this arrangement, because they can develop a closer and more understanding relationship with their teachers, and have the opportunity to get to know them as individuals, away from the classroom situation. There is often time for conversation in a club, or for having a Coke together. This may accomplish wonders with boys or girls who need to identify with an adult, and do not often get the chance. By the same token, the teacher will gain a deeper understanding of the children, their talents, and their problems and their needs.

For teachers who have outside interests, the student activities program, through the clubs, the evening school, and the trips, can help them to utilize their knowledge. We knew of one teacher, for example, who is licensed to teach social studies, but who is also an expert in the area of Far Eastern culture, and teaches a course in Chinese in the evening school. Physical fitness may be taught not only by physical education teachers, but by any person interested in this area. This is true of many other fields of knowledge. Many teachers will be working in their own subject areas, but extracurricular work may encourage them to learn as much as they can, to go into greater depth in their own fields—or in related areas. A case in point is a young science teacher who became fascinated in oceanography, and who then ran a club for boys and girls as a result of his further study, and consequent specialization in this field.

You will probably find, among the members of your staff, many people who are able to teach contract bridge, chess or any of the hobby areas. It is wise for you to utilize their talents, and, of course, make them financially remunerative. For work in the career areas, the guidance staff should be employed, since their background and studies will add to the program immeasurably, particularly as they delve deeply into the topics for club or evening school discussion.

Many aspects of this program help to develop leadership qualities among the faculty. The person who coaches teams, the advisor of the general organization, the director of the evening school, all must learn administration, and this is particularly fine on-the-job-training. Furthermore, it may have a decided effect on the teacher's personality. The shy, sensitive, diffident teacher, sometimes unsure of herself and her capabilities, when thrown into an administrative capacity may suddenly achieve a delightful self-assurance. Her pedagogical powers may increase, and instead of being withdrawn, she may become more outgoing toward her children and her colleagues, as a result of this experience.

Having shown the teachers that they will personally benefit by supporting the program, our next problem is instructing them in doing this. Here are some suggestions:

PROMOTING THE STUDENT ACTIVITIES PROGRAM WITHIN THE SCHOOL

1) A simple matter of getting notices home to the parents can be very critical—for if people do not know about a program, how can they take part in it? If a parent is not informed about a club, how can he encourage his youngster to join it? If an adult is not aware of the evening school opportunities, how will he enroll in it? The teacher must distribute the materials, remind the children to give them to their parents, and then collect the returns when a response is requested.

2) The boys and girls must be kept informed of the affairs of the school. These should be discussed in their classrooms, and the activities of the Student Government be covered in full. They should be made aware of the happenings in the school—and also in the community. If there is an event-of-the-year, it should be discussed at great length, for, without developing involvement and enthusiasm, much of its value is lost.

3) Each class should elect class officers, and they should actually function in the classroom situation. By fostering this, the

teacher is helping to strengthen the children's concepts of democratic processes, for they are really living them. He is therefore helping the development of future citizens. If a teacher does not bother to do this, if he is reluctant to turn over *some* of the reins of government, then his children lose out in valuable experiential learning. When children run their own affairs, they become intensely interested and enthused.

4) In the student activities program, each department is often called upon, and its teachers given additional opportunities. This is evident in the publication of the literary magazine or the newspaper, which require contributions from the language arts and art departments. But teachers of social studies and science, of foreign language and mathematics should be encouraged to contribute the work of their classes, as well. A well-written article in any subject area which is worth printing should find its rightful place in the school publication. Assignments, which involve creative work in the field, should be considered. When children are told their work may be published, the quality will improve. If they are guided by their teachers this improvement is almost guaranteed. The publications should represent the combined talents of all the departments.

5) If each teacher who leads a club announces it to his classes, asks them for suggestions, and takes them into consideration when he does his planning, the club membership will grow. If the teacher is a stimulating person, and if he paints a picture of a series of club activities the children will find exciting, boys and girls will seek membership in his club. Often young people will become interested in new fields as a result of their association with exciting personalities. Teachers should be encouraged to take the children into their confidence, to ask the boys and girls what would really appeal to them, and then to try to utilize this information.

It is obvious that they would not find Chaucer to their taste— unless the person handling the literary club was very, very skillful. Mentioning "Catcher in the Rye," would immediately captivate many, many more students even if the teacher were not so great. If an unfortunate choice is made, one the children would dislike because it is beyond their comprehension, a love of literature—one of the objectives of our profession, would definitely be defeated.

The teacher who can take his clues, and his direction from the young people will be far more successful in anything he attempts—be it teaching his classes, supervising the Student Government, or leading a club. In the evening school, it is the needs of the students which must be given first consideration.

6) The student activities program can benefit from salesmanship and good promotion.

One of the best means of promotion of extracurricular activities is through assembly programs. Here is the opportunity to spell out what is being done in the various aspects of the student activities program. For example, the officers of the Student Government should report regularly on the work they are doing and on its progress. A special day should be devoted to clubs, with announcements by the officers of each club, outlining the activities the club is engaged in, and the members reactions to them. Honesty should be encouraged, for if every club is the "greatest," the audience may become skeptical. The members should be the salesmen, in the assembly situation, rather than faculty advisors. The audience should be encouraged to take notes, and invitations should be issued to them, inviting them to join, and telling them when and where the club meets.

Club members should not be overburdened, but they should, at the same time, have enough to do to hold and further their interest. This may be accomplished by trips, speakers, research projects, discussion. Then this should be followed by recording some of the results in newspapers or magazine articles, photographs and tape recordings to keep as mementos. If the club leader is passive, and really does nothing worthy of note, both he and the club lose out.

Teachers should be encouraged to make every activity in the extracurricular program self-motivating. Young people will, if given the starting points and the responsibility, rise to the occasion. They often need direction, and their judgment may not be the best, but once started on the track, they will complete the tasks that they have assigned to themselves. If the leader of the Stamp Club asks the members to prepare booklets of duplicate stamps for distribution to patients in hospitals, he may have to give one or two more directions, but the youngsters will do the rest—on their own. He may choose, rather, to ask for suggestions in regard to what to do with the duplicates, and allow the members to work this problem out for themselves. The boys and girls will, if consulted and encouraged to become self-directing, develop and grow to meet the needs of the occasion. A leader should not be too strong, but should be in the background, giving guidance when needed.

7) The Parents Association should be kept informed of all of the aspects of the extracurricular program—from the work of the Student Government to the clubs, the teams, and every other activity. This should be part of a report given to them either monthly, or at least bimonthly. The student activities program involves extra funding, and they should be aware of what the money is being spent for, and what the results of its expenditure are. In this way, the Parents Association may become one of the staunchest supporters of this program. The members should get to see the resulting newspapers put out by the clubs, should be invited to take part in the trips scheduled, should go to the ball games the teams play, and should be considered an integral part of the program.

They should also discuss the program from its most important vantage point—how are their children benefiting from it. Are they enthused? Are they taking part? What are their reactions? If children are unaware of the activities going on in the school, if they are uninterested in taking part, the Parents Association should speak up, for feedback from them must be considered to be very important.

You may wish to have the leaders of the various activities address the parent groups, or the children may do so. If you choose to try the latter, have the teachers or directors in attendance, to offer extra information, when necessary, and to be available for questions and for comments. Nothing is more frustrating for a parent than to be told by her child, "Mr. Smith says I can't join his club," and then not be able to find Mr. Smith to check up on this. Usually she would find that Mr. Smith had said, "I don't see how you can join a photography club, if you are already a member of the baseball club, and they both meet on the same day." The face-to-face discussion is much easier than long, drawn out efforts to communicate, and should be taken advantage of, whenever possible.

8) Exhibits should be set up, within the school, and preferably in the main lobby, showing the student activities program in action. This may be done by displaying the newspapers or magazines the clubs produce, by mounting and labeling the photographs of the various activities, and by having on display some of the products of the clubs or the evening school. The regular work of the students, in their classes, should be displayed in the classrooms, and on the bulletin boards throughout the school.

These displays serve as actual means of communication that make students, faculty and parents aware of the happenings in the extracurricular program.

Photographs of any concerts, plays or other performances should be in evidence, as well as snapshots of the event-of-the-year. The literary magazine, school newspaper, and any other publications should have places of honor, for these, too, result from the student activities program. The latter also serve by entering the homes of many of the students, and by being read, and reread by the youngsters.

HOBBY DISPLAYS

Once a year, a display of hobbies may be set up—including those of the teachers, students and parents. This has proven to be a highly successful endeavor, with a multiplicity of activities represented. We have used this device in conjunction with the Winter Festival, and it has proved to be a very popular attraction. It included handiwork such as beading and embroidery, painting and sculpture, handcrafted furniture and mosaics. Also on display were recordings made by one language arts teacher, who is also a musician, pictures in stamps, ceramics, photographs, slides, clothing and many, many other items. Because this represented the work of everyone in any way connected with the school, and because everyone was invited to participate, the reaction was a most enthusiastic one. Not only that, but here, too, children realized that their teachers had many talents. Their mathematics teacher, they learned, for instance, proved to be a professional photographer, as well.

It should be the task of all of the leaders of the students activities programs to bring to the children as many new interests as possible. This broadening of horizons may be done in a variety of ways:

By visiting other clubs, children see the work going on in them, taste the samples available—literally or figuratively and determine which suit them. A boy who has been playing baseball should be introduced to golf. A girl who has been sewing may find she becomes interested in collecting stamps. The system of cross-pollination may be furthered by setting up specific days when clubs will cross visit.

Another way to bring new interests to children is through the evening school. There should surely be open-school nights, when the boys and girls are invited to visit, and to see the work being done in the various courses. While youngsters in elementary school are too young to attend, they are very receptive to new ideas, and to new subjects. The child hearing Chinese for the first time may be fascinated, and motivated to learn it. Often such motivation persists for years. Crafts attract the attention of boys and girls, and an evening set aside for experimentation for everyone helps to introduce them to each other, and at the same time may serve as an impetus for adults to register for the course, the next time it is given.

The trips taken as part of the club program offer many possibilities of new interests for children. They need not be expensive or to far-away places to have this effect. For city children, if you can provide them with a walk in the woods in winter, or along the seashore on a bleak fall day, you can stimulate ideas, and bring out talent which lay dormant before this.

The child who does his first piece of ceramics in the ceramics club is thrilled. The boy whose touchdown wins the game remembers this forever. All of these, and many more experiences are brought to the children in the students activities program. The teachers and leaders are the people, however, who make the program important to the child, and who might make it an interesting part of his life. If the club meeting is fun, if practice for the team is stimulating, if the enthusiasm of the cheerleaders is felt by the crowd, these are truly memorable experiences for the children. But it can be the attitude of the adults, themselves, which makes the important difference between an experience, and a great experience.

REMUNERATION FOR TEACHERS

There is no question, but that we must include payment for teachers, if they are asked to work after school hours in the student activities program. Adequate remuneration is surely deserved, and the days of teachers working for three hours a day, after school, for several days a week at a salary of a few hundred dollars a year are over, and have been for a number of years. As professionals, using their skills, teachers should be paid at rates which are commensurate with their abilities. The extra work often entails expenditures of additional time for preparation, and it also involves a good deal of dedication to the youngsters. If we wish to make the student activities program one of the strong points of the school's offerings, we must be willing to include this added expense in our budgetary considerations, for, as we have stated throughout this book, the extracurricular areas are as important to the children's development as the hours they spend in the classrooms, and, in many cases, even more important. The funds spent for the program will, you will find, be money well spent—if your program is an effective one.

How to Effectively   **12**
Involve Parents in
the Student Activities
Program

In our book, "Successful Methods for Teaching the Slow Learner," we refer to the parents as the "essential ally." This alliance is as necessary in regard to the student activities program as it is in connection with the teaching program. Parents, today, are clamouring for a say in the running of the schools, and it ill behooves us to ignore their voices. By involving them in our extracurricular programs they are given the opportunities to make valid and real contributions to the intellectual growth of their children, to the improvement of the educational program of the school, and to the climate established in the building. With these factors in mind, how can we go about making these parents our allies? How can we invite them into our schools, and how can we work together?

BRINGING THE PARENTS INTO THE SCHOOL

There are a myriad of ways in which the parents can be invited to contribute to the extracurricular program of the school. One of the most effective ways is to invite them to be club leaders. If you decide to do this, we suggest you have a training program for them, in which you stress the elements of good leadership, some of which are outlined in Chapter 5. For those who have been den mothers, for the Boy or Girl Scouts, this training may be lessened or omitted completely. However, the basic concepts of club management should be reviewed with everyone. If possible, invite fathers as well as mothers to lead clubs, for very often, it is the male image which is lacking in the lives of some of the children, and a club situation is an excellent place to supply it. The informality of the organization makes this preferable to a classroom, and a boy who has no father may be able to relate to the leader of his club, thereby fulfilling a very important need in the child's life.

Parents are often able to lead many of the clubs which are non-academic in orientation. It is the task of the principal, and the supervisor in charge of the club program, to interview the applicants, and screen them carefully, to make sure they understand the basic philosophy of education and of life espoused by the school. If the school philosophy is based on flexibility, a rigid person would hardly fit in. For instance, there are adults who feel children should be seen and not heard, and these would be disastrous in any aspect of the club program.

Parents may be invited as guest speakers on a number of occasions. They may address the assemblies, or the clubs, the Student Government or the classes. People in various professions may be invited to discuss their work; travelers may be asked to describe their trips, possibly with movie film or slide accompaniment. Professionals in the entertainment field may be asked to perform for the boys and girls. Parents with interesting hobbies and avocations are often requested to share them with young people, and relatives of the students who are with bands or orchestras, folk singers or singing groups, may wish to contribute to the pleasure of the youngsters by performing for them.

While in some cases, parents may feel the requests from the school (which should be handwritten by boys and girls—who are officers of Student Government or of the clubs,) are an imposition, in most cases the recipients are honored, and pleased to accept.

Advisors are needed for the athletic teams, and for the cheerleaders, and, if faculty members are not trained to handle this, it is possible to find parents, or adult members of the community

—Official Photograph, Board of Education, City of New York

PARENTS PERFORMING BEFORE A YOUTHFUL AUDIENCE

who are qualified to do so. A good coach is vital to the success of any team, and a person outside of the school faculty may be able to do a better job than one who works with the children in the capacity of teacher as well.

In the after school tutorial program, parents are more than welcome, particularly when they work on a one-to-one basis with the children. Because it requires a large number of people, this type of program is often staffed by volunteers. We have found it to be highly successful. The volunteer teachers need training, of course, as much or more than the club leaders, and it is essential that it be arranged for before the program is initiated. The after school tutorial program can mean a great deal to the youngsters—particularly if they have difficulty with any of their subjects. We have seen it have a dramatic effect on children who have low opinions of themselves, and are not certain of their ability to learn. Others, who wish to learn such subjects as typing, will appreciate it equally as much.

Parents may take part in trips, and are often counted upon, to help with the supervision of youngsters, when they are away from the protective atmosphere of the school building. Very often plans for a trip are discarded because there is no parent willing to take part. In some schools, in order to avoid this possibility, two class mothers are selected or elected from among those who volunteer for this task. By assuming the duties of the Class Mother, a woman promises to go on any trips the class is scheduled to take— or to supply a substitute for herself. The Class Mother may have other duties, depending on the role assigned to her at the beginning of the year.

In the publication of the school newspaper or literary magazine, it may be necessary to find a person willing to type or to illustrate, to do lay-outs or work on advertising. Parents are very often capable of doing this, and enjoy doing it. We know of one mother, whose husband's yearly income was in six figures, but who looked forward to typing the school newspaper each month in preparation for publication.

In productions, parents can assist in an unlimited number of ways. They may assist with the direction, and with the make-up, and are often counted upon to make the costumes. It has been our experience that, no matter how many families with severe financial problems an area has, there is always money for costumes. Mothers are happy to make these, and will use remnants and dyed gauze, if need be, but when their children appear on the stage, they are properly dressed for the occasion. We have asked for help in scenery design and painting, and been rewarded with creations—far superior to what was expected.

For the event-of-the-year, there are many roles the parents may assume—although usually this is one evening when they should be considered the honored guests. We have had the festivities photographed by fathers, and tape recorded by mothers, and been represented in the local press by happy visitors.

In the evening school program, while many of the students are members of the parents of the school population, others may act in the capacity of instructors. The expert accountant may lead the group learning to do its own income tax returns, and the registered nurse may teach the baby-sitting course. The commercial artist, the linguist or the athlete may be able to contribute his talents to this program. By having members of the community on both sides of the desks, an atmosphere of camaraderie may develop which is devoutly to be desired.

HELPING IN THE IMPORTANT DECISION MAKING

We believe that parents must be involved in many of the decisions which affect their children. By meeting with the Parents Association, and discussing problems with them, many difficulties may be averted. For example, in working out the series of courses to be offered in the evening school, what is the feeling of the parents in regard to a course in driver's education? Do they want it to be given? What about sex education and family living? Is it possible that they would prefer this in a club situation, rather than in a course in school. In the evening school which languages should be offered, and what type of models would be used in the art classes?

The avenues of communication between the principal, the entire staff and representatives of the parents, (usually in the form of the Parents or Parent Teacher's Association) must be kept open. Parents should feel free to consult with the administration, and with the teachers whenever they deem necessary. This manifestation of mutual respect is a must. Without it, the strongest school will flounder. When the principal must discuss a matter with the parents, if he and the executive board of the Parents Association have a working relationship, the problem is far nearer to solution. He may consult with them to learn their thinking on the subject, and then he is able to proceed from knowledge, rather than on a blind.

In establishing the student activities program, consultation of this type is very valuable, for the principal may not be "tuned-in" to the homelife of the children, and may not be aware of the problems they, and their parents face. For example, if graduation exercises and a prom are planned, and each child is required to spend ten dollars, are the parents able and willing to make this expenditure? Will the parents permit their children to remain in school after school hours? Cooperation is the keynote, and, as we said, the parent is the essential ally.

WORKING TO BENEFIT
THE SCHOOL AND THE COMMUNITY

The parents are in a position to do a great deal of constructive work in behalf of the entire community. If they have an organization, this may function in their dealings with local officials. We have seen parent groups work for a community swimming pool, and have the pleasure of seeing one built in half the time it usually takes, as a result of the pressure they brought to bear.

Additional police, crossing guards, and even detectives have been placed near schools, through the efforts of the parents. Additional sanitation men have been assigned to specific areas, in response to parental requests. The formation of parent groups is one way to change things, if there are feelings that they ought to be changed.

Often there is philanthropic work which can be done by parent organizations to better the area in which they live. Working with groups of young people in old-age or nursing homes has proved highly successful, and a boon to the residents of these institutions. Neighborhood clean-up campaigns have had extremely good results, and these are often instituted by the school, or by the parent association.

Within each school, almost regardless of the area in which it is located, there are often children who need clothing. Parents have set up "stores" in which these children, inconspicuously, have been able to select skirts or blouses, pants or shirts. The supplies come from the outgrown clothes of their own youngsters. Excess clothing may be sent to those sections of our country, such as Appalachia, where the need for it is very great. Parents have often run clothing drives to accumulate a large assortment of apparel, which is then sent to places where it will be put to good use. It is wise to involve the Student Government in this type of endeavor. Roy Rogers and Dale Evans have, for many years, been involved in this philanthropy, a most worthwhile one.

At Christmas time, toys may be collected, and restored or repaired. This activity, also involving the Student Government, is a boon to every housewife who has rummage she would like to get rid of, particularly those items which are too good to throw away. For the "saver" this type of collection is welcomed with open arms.

Parents have worked with young people to supply toys for children in local hospitals as well. If your parent groups are interested in community service, they can do great things—and working with the children of the school, teaches the youngsters a great deal, as well.

LIAISON WITH THE LOCAL GOVERNMENT OFFICIALS

As has been pointed out, the Parents Association, working with elected officials, carries far greater weight than the principal and the staff of a school. The reason is simple—the parents control far more votes than does the principal. For this reason, in dealing with civil servants, the parents should do the dealing, and the principal will find it possible to accomplish things he may never have dreamed of, with their aid and support.

MORAL SUPPORT FOR THE TEACHERS

Every human being seeks acceptance and approbation—from the highest to the most lowly—from the octogenarian to the two year old. Our teachers are no exception, and seek manifestations of approval. Parents show their moral support of their teachers by their interest and concern. Meeting a parent in the halls, and hearing her say, "I am so grateful for Mr. X. He made my son love science, and he even explained the computer to him," often will make the principal's day, and impress him with the teacher's ability.

When parents are thrown into contact with the teachers, and are able to speek freely to them, the moral support the teachers seek is often forthcoming. There is need for such situations to be structured. These may be at formal meetings, but far more effective are the informal situations which arise when people work together.

By inviting parents to participate in the student activities program, in any of its many facets, the parents are brought into contact with the teachers. They find the opportunities to discuss things which are troubling them, but also to learn about their children, and to become more closely acquainted with the teachers.

The parents, if given frequent opportunities to become involved with the school, will identify with it, and be far less apt to criticize. They should surely share in the major events, and the important occasions. One cannot picture graduation exercises without an audience of mothers and fathers, grandmothers and grandfathers. Yet, why not include some of these relatives on the stage, as participants in the program, as well? When there are parties, or proms, dances or dinners, shouldn't parents share in these happy times? They are usually willing to work very dilligently for their children, and we have seen them laboring long and hard on some of the projects undertaken by the Parents' Association or the Parent-Teachers group. Let us suggest an event which the children "throw" for their parents.

The Children's Dinner

This event might be a Father-Daughter Dinner, a Mother-Son Luncheon, a Family Evening or any variation thereof.

Have the representatives of the Student Government decide on the type of affair they wish. Try to point out that, if they make one for the fathers, there should be another for the mothers. A full family party takes these factors into consideration. (You may find it necessary to supply a baby-sitting service. One or two of the clubs might be able to cope with this.)

Choose a time of year when people are not busy. From Thanksgiving through New Year's everyone seems rushed—and so, while holiday parties are very pleasant, to many parents they become burdens because they cannot spare the time. February is a far better choice, or March—but not immediately before Easter. In the fall, get acquainted gatherings can be an important event in the community and may be held in late September, October or early November.

Let us stress one point. These parties should be planned and completely produced by the children. Of course, with fifth graders there is need for far more supervision than with older children, but even 11 year olds will surprise you with their efforts. We suggest you give them the opportunity. The planning will be a great part of the fun, and the actual party a joy. This cannot help but have a wonderful effect on your school-community relation.

Use your gymnasium, or cafeteria. Have the children select a theme, and decorate accordingly. Valentine's Day or Lincoln's Birthday comes to mind because this makes the decor and even the menu so simple to plan. Set up tables and chairs (easily rented) and have a buffet dinner. The children (stress—not the parents this time) should prepare some of the foods. (Perhaps with guidance from mothers of course.) Cold cuts can be arranged on trays, by the girls and boys. If any faculty members enjoy cooking they may wish to contribute their talents. Desserts should be spectacular—flaming cherries jubilee, for example, or cherry pie a la mode. But—the youngsters must select the menu, and be responsible for the entire production.

Who pays for this? Each child who can afford it, will be happy to contribute—and, by fixing the price at slightly higher than necessary, some will absorb the costs for others less fortunate. If your school is affluent, perhaps you will decide to foot the bill yourself. Wonderful! If money is a problem, a candy sale can be run to raise funds. We have raised thousands of dollars in a relatively short time by this device.

A function of this sort should be run by committees, involving as many pupils as possible. For example, the following committees might be used. The finance committee would determine the budget, and pay the bills. There should be a welcoming committee, an entertainment committee and five food and drink committees: (1) appetizers and salads, (2) main dishes, (3) breads and cakes (4) desserts and (5) drinks. Instead of having a clean up committee, have each of these groups clean up its own contributions. You may wish to have background music (*not* rock and roll, but soft, pleasant show tunes for example). That decision leads to the establishment of a music committee. Photographs may be taken—another committee. Add your own ideas—and those of the children to this list.

Here, as always, enthusiasm is the keynote. This should be a joyous occasion. By overburdening no one, by sharing responsibility—and by adequate time and preparation, this can easily be a huge success. You may wish to break this down into grade affairs. In a junior high or high school, with 700 children per grade, even that may be too many. In that case, divide the grade, and hold each party separately.

There will be need for faculty advisors to work with the children —particularly in the estimation of the amount of food necessary. Books may be consulted, and research done by the committees.

Such an occasion as this provides the impetus for fun, and part of any such affair should be skits and games, parodies or productions (though not of a grand nature). Simple potato or relay races, square dancing or folk singing are appropriate and pleasant.

This is the type of thing which will, if repeated, yearly grow and grow, as new ideas are suggested. But never allow it to change its essential characteristic—of children doing something for their parents.

WORKING TO RAISE MONEY
FOR SPECIAL EXTRA PROGRAMS

Parents' organizations have raised funds in many ways. Book fairs have been highly successful, and incidentally encouraged children to read. Many commercial firms will assist you in setting up the entire sale. Your mothers supply the labor—and make no mistakes, there is a great deal of work involved.

Cake and candy sales, in the cafeteria, are often run, with profits well worth the time and effort invested.

There are schools where parents run plant sales, especially around Mother's Day. These are highly successful, and a real help to the children, for they can do their shopping conveniently, and usually with a minimum of expense.

We mentioned a candy sale, and will discuss it here in detail. Your parents' organization may wish to run one, working with the students. Ours was truly sensational! Here are some of the details. We alluded to this sale before, implying it was on a large scale. It was! The children did the actual selling, and what a job they did! There are many commercial companies which will aid you, as they did us, in this endeavor. They suggested simple motivational devices which proved very effective. The candy was sold for one dollar a box, and each box sold was credited to the child. When he had sold his first twelve boxes, he was given one ticket for a drawing for a television set. Then, for every six additional boxes he sold, he received another ticket. Furthermore, in addition to the drawing, the youngster selling the most boxes in the entire school would get a $25 prize, and the five runners up would each get $5. A number of children sold over one hundred boxes of candy, and the winners (there were two tied for first place—each sold over 180). It was a pleasure, too, to see one of these hard workers win the drawing for the television set. Every child in the assembly cheered. We felt, though, that one of the most important aspects of this was the beneficial effect it had on the spirit of the school, and the cooperative atmosphere which pervaded the entire project. Should you decide to run such a sale, be sure the candy is good. Ours was excellent, and we were our own frequent customers. How many pounds were gained that week!

Your parents may decide to give the children the candy on credit. We required our youngsters to pay for it before they received it—so they had to take orders in advance. Some of the young entrepreneurs used their own capital to buy the candy, and then sold it. They claimed sales were simpler, that way. Each box had a school label on it, showing it was being used for fund raising.

Our sale was run the ten days before Easter. We sold the incredible amount of over nine thousand boxes of candy, and the profits were in excess of $3,300. This made funds available for many things we heretofore could not afford. It also, incidentally, brought out the business talent of many youngsters, which had previously been completely hidden.

Books, or gifts, "white elephants" or antiques, there are many ways to raise funds, and at the same time supply an atmosphere of camaraderie to parents and children, faculty and community. Then, too, adults as well as children need to feel satisfaction, and this sort of endeavor is a marvelous way of fulfilling this need.

HELPING INDIVIDUAL CHILDREN WITHIN THE SCHOOL

Parents may work with children, in a one-to-one relationship, in reading clinics, or in other areas. There are children who require an inordinate amount of attention, and this type of situation is very effective with such children. Their gains in reading may be incidental to their gains in development. Of course, for parents willing to take on this sort of responsibility, training is essential before they can work with any child. We suggest it be training in reading skills, and also in child development and psychology, so that they become aware of any problems the child may have. There should be a guidance person available, too, for consultation and discussion of the children—for very often the child with learning problems has other problems as well.

Individual instruction in art, for children with talent, may be given by parents who are qualified in this area. Music, too, might be taught in this way.

If there are many adults who are willing to do this individualized type of teaching, we believe that work on handwriting, and on writing skills can be of tremendous value. Some children show great difficulty in grasping the concept of the sentence, and working with them on this may prove most worthwhile. A child may have been taught a concept many, many times, but not master it until it is taught in a one-to-one relationship, with a highly personal approach.

The parents who seek to involve themselves in this teaching situation must be warm, interested individuals. An unresponsive person, not "tuned in" to the children's needs, will be, at best, unsuccessful, and might, if permitted to do so, do more damage than good. Screening the applicants carefully is a must. The supervisor must get over the idea that every volunteer is able to teach. This simply is not true. The volunteer may be used in other capacities, but not necessarily in working with children.

The School as a Social   13
and Sociological Center

There is no aware person in the world who can deny the fact that times are changing, and changing so rapidly as to be almost unbelievable. We are living in an era characterized by nothing as much as change. Our schools are caught up in the tide, and we must adjust our programs and offerings to meet the needs of the community and of the adults, as well as the students. We have accused college people of having lived in ivory towers, but, we, too, have been somewhat isolated from the mainstream. There have been needs of which we have not been aware, and youngsters, whom we have rejected, crying for help. This rejection has not been a personal matter, but rather an institutional one. The same is true of our relationships with parents. It is essential that we review our practices and procedures in view of the changing times, and rededicate our schools to a new philosophy—based on the philosophy of community service. The student activities program is geared to this, and lends itself to many adaptations and new ideas. Let us pursue some of them.

SUPPLYING A HOME
AWAY FROM HOME FOR THE CHILDREN

For many years the schools closed their doors at three or four o'clock. It closed them to those children with no one waiting for them at home and no place to go, but to an empty house. It is true there are many more mothers working today than ever before, but there were still, years ago, in the lower economic segment of our population, women working to support their families. What are the schools doing today to help solve the problem of caring for these children of working mothers? Provision should be made for these children. The child is in the school building. Shouldn't we supply a place for him to remain—a home away from home? In the student activities program this is done—by means of after-school

—Official Photograph, Board of Education, City of New York

SHARING—ONE OF THE PRIMARY PLEASURES OF LIFE

study halls and clubs, game rooms and teams, and evening school programs. A youngster may remain in the building, with supervision, for many additional hours.

If your school is in an area which has many working mothers, and few facilities for young people, is it possible for you to consider instituting a program which would supply dinners and a place for young people to remain gainfully employed, or socializing, reading or watching television, until it is time for them to go to bed? Is this concept too Utopian, too much ahead of its time? It is entirely feasible, but, of course, requires a great deal in the way of funding. If this is too "far-out," can you consider opening the doors to them, without the provision of the meal? You have the space, and the equipment. Of course the question is where do you get the staff? Yet, in the future, something of this nature must be done—because the needs for it are so great, so undeniable.

WELCOMING THE MEMBERS OF THE COMMUNITY

We have listed a number of ways in which the parents may be made to feel welcome in the school. Many of these are applicable to members of the community as well. For example, many may be asked to speak to the children at assemblies, or as part of the program of the careers club. In extending the invitations, which should be written by the children, the phrasing should be such that the person can refuse the invitation gracefully, if he must do so. For example, if a busy physician, or businessman is invited to speak, the letter might read,

"Dear Dr. X" or "Dear Mr. Y."

"Our Careers Club would like to invite you to take part in our meeting on September 25, at 3:30 p.m. You will be the featured speaker. After your talk we are sure the members will have questions, and we like to allow time for this. Since our meetings end by 5:00 p.m. you can judge your time accordingly.

"We realize that your schedule is a very busy one, and should you have to refuse our invitation, or postpone your appearance until a more favorable date, we will understand perfectly. Thank you for your consideration."

Notices of the happenings in the school may be sent to community centers; these may be printed in the form of posters, which are usually hung on bulletin boards used for the purpose. To invite the community, such notices should also appear in the local newspaper. This media of communication should be utilized when the staffing is being done, for the after school tutorial program, for the club leaders, or for the evening school. Announcements should be made to the colleges in the areas, as well, for many students may be interested in this type of work.

There are often times when the members of the community might like to visit a school, but feel reluctant to do so. How can you hang out the "Welcome" mat? One way is to offer tours of the building. In one school we know of, these are given every Friday morning, Friday having been chosen because it is the most unquiet day of the week. These tours are conducted by the principal, or one of his assistants, and usually take about one and one-half to two hours. Visitors are shown the entire school plant, and taken into many classrooms, the library, auditorium and even the cafeteria. Youngsters are encouraged to speak to them in the halls. The officers of the Student Government are on hand to take over the tour direction at times. The reactions of the guests are invariably favorable. Tours may be publicized in the local newspaper, offered to community groups, and other organizations. Schools as well as times have changed, and most of our schools are very different today from what they were even twenty years ago. Those members of the community who do not have children or grandchildren attending them find it difficult to comprehend this difference, and it is to the advantage of the school to interpret it to and for them.

We would like to go one giant step forward, and suggest the use of the school building and facilities for our senior citizens.

GOLDEN AGE CLUBS IN OUR SCHOOLS

The number of senior citizens in our nation is increasing at a tremendous rate. With almost unbelievable advances in medicine, people are living longer, but many are finding little to do which is worthwhile or rewarding. With this in mind, we suggest the establishment of a center for the senior citizens in every high school, and in many elementary schools. Because most of these people are not employed, many of them live on their pensions, or on the money they receive from Social Security. They are therefore limited in their expenditures—one cannot do very much if one receives an income of $64 per month. If centers for these people were established in neighborhood schools, they would not have to travel to them, but could walk, thus saving their limited funds for other uses. Our schools are fully utilized from nine to three, and afterward many of the rooms are empty. These could be devoted to the Golden Age Center, along with those facilities which are not needed for other purposes.

Retired people are, of course, eligible for evening school, but even the token registration fee is probably too much for them to pay. Should we not, even now, without the Golden Age Clubs in our schools, permit them to register for such courses, free of charge, if money is a problem to them?

We should encourage our senior citizens to do tutoring, if they are capable of this, assist on trips, and make any contributions they can. However, in the majority of cases we must reach out to them, for many of them are alone, and afraid. They need friends to identify with, game rooms and places for get-togethers. Our Golden Age Centers need not be separate from the rest of the school, but may be an important adjunct to it. If space is limited, they may meet in the cafeteria, after it has been used during the children's lunch hours. If this is impractical, they may meet after three, when the building is less utilized. Staffing should be provided by the community, or the project may be started, and planned to eventually become self-sustaining. We know of one such center which has a food concession, and this small coffee shop has contributed to the financial operation of the center and given the members many pleasant hours. As one spry little old lady told us, "Now I don't have to eat my breakfast alone. You don't know how important that is to me!"

FOSTERING THE EXCHANGE OF IDEAS

In the colleges, lounges serve many functions. They are a meeting place for students, and for students and teachers. We propose a variation of this be adopted for the high schools. By setting up a place where people can get together after school for a cup of coffee or hot chocolate, and for conversation, we encourage our students to socialize with other students in the school, and with some of the adults as well. Why not call it the "Collegiate Lounge," and serve just the two items mentioned? This may even be done by vending machine, and the return from the machines would probably pay the salary of the person supervising. There must be supervision, of course, but by someone to whom the children can relate, whom they like, and who enjoys them. Teachers should be encouraged to drop in, but not forced to do so. If the atmosphere is pleasant, many of the young members of the staff will take advantage of the opportunity to sit around and talk.

Conversation is almost a lost art in the United States. One has but to visit Europe, and sit in sidewalk cafes to appreciate what we have missed. By establishing a lounge, perhaps we can introduce it to our young people.

The Student Government should be influential in operating this lounge, and should keep it decorated and clean. This may mean employing people to do the work, or appointing committees to handle it. Pictures of the students make attractive decoration, and are even more interesting after they have graduated, and are no longer in the school.

We mentioned the possibility of a concession in terms of the Golden Age Center, and the same is true in the case of the lounge. Or it may be operated, as we said, by the boys and girls themselves, for this is an excellent way to develop responsibility. The lounge may be housed in a separate area, or may be in one part of the cafeteria, screened off, so that it is more cosy and intimate than a huge dining hall.

One of the colleges with which we are familiar has used its lounge to great advantage. It shows films there—always carefully chosen, and stimulating. After the showing, there are discussion groups, small rather than large, and the film is thoroughly discussed by the young people. It has proved to be an eminently successful program, which has attracted high school students, as well as the students of the college. This might easily be copied by high schools, with the same admission price charged—usually one dollar. It serves the children, and, at the same time, raises funds for the Student Government. Concerts, and folk singing are also possible programs, which have proved very successful in the colleges. Our young people need this type of place to congregate and this opportunity for entertainment. Far too often there is little of interest available to them, and they turn to other ways to spend their leisure time, ways which may prove harmful or dangerous. The lounge may be set up anywhere, at almost any time, and with a very small investment. Films may be shown for meager sums. Is this idea not worth a trial—if your community needs it?

BRIDGING THE GENERATION GAP

In order to bridge the generation gap, we need to open avenues of communication, which so often are closed, between youngsters

—Official Photograph, Board of Education, City of New York

PRINCIPAL AND STUDENTS CONFER

and their parents, and other adult members of the community. The establishment of the lounge may be one way to do this. If films are shown, and discussion groups set up, many people should be invited, parents as well as youngsters. The lounge supplies a place for sitting around and talking; if adults and boys and girls congregate, there is bound to be some conversation.

Working on projects together is an excellent means of building relationships. A toy repair project is a particularly good one, for this purpose. Dressing dolls may be added to this, and even the collection of books. Youngsters should collect the items and the actual repair work done by both children and adults. They will, therefore have to sit down to work together—and conversation will inevitably follow.

If there is a Golden Age Center, the young people may serve as waiters and waitresses, and through the clubs, tournaments in chess and checkers may be held, as well as bridge games. In certain skill areas, such as cooking, the other generations have much to contribute to the boys and girls. Sewing and knitting skills may be taught, with individual attention given, to some of the young people by the adults. Cooking is another area in which experience is of tremendous value, and learning to cook from a person who is an expert offers a tremendous opportunity to the right child.

By baby sitting, the boys and girls become acquainted with adults living in their area, and may develop relationships with them. We feel that when we invite both parents to a school function, a baby sitting service should be sponsored by the Student Government and housed right in the school building. Far too many parents cannot attend such functions, concerts or plays— because of the lack of a person to care for their young children.

BRINGING CULTURAL PURSUITS
TO THE ENTIRE COMMUNITY

In many communities there is no organized effort to provide programs of cultural interest to the public, and therefore nothing is accomplished in this area. The television set serves as the focus of entertainment for most people, with perhaps a movie once a week.

There is no reason why the local school cannot assume part of this responsibility. If your school is located in a large city, you may find that, in spite of the fact that there are many attractions available, people do not avail themselves of these opportunities. They are not sufficiently motivated, and so they stay in their own backyards. But, more important, a program of this nature will enrich the lives of our boys and girls, will introduce them to many new and exciting experiences, and is certainly the logical outgrowth of the student activities program.

In establishing a series of evening entertainments, do not be discouraged if you get off to a slow start. Lethargy and that TV set may defeat your purpose. If you start with programs which appeal to the young adults as well as the boys and girls, they will be very well attended. We recall one evening of poetry reading (Kahlil Gibran) and sitar music. The large auditorium was completely filled.

You may initiate an entertainment series by possibly polling the parents' organization and/or the community to determine what types of programs they would be interested in seeing. We will discuss many offerings and from these you may offer a choice of type. When you learn what the public's pleasure is, you can contact booking agents, and touring companies. We suggest you keep the fees to a minimum. If you accept the assumption that this program has a very important purpose—in terms of introducing our young people to cultural pursuits, then you will plan with the idea in mind that the admission fees should pay for the performance, but that substantial profits should not be sought. If the program becomes very popular, then the price of admissions may be increased—but not for the students.

You may wish to poll your youngsters, too, to determine their likes and dislikes. However, the purpose of this is not to introduce them to the music they love, but to bring them new and different interests. We have watched youngsters held absolutely spellbound, by a performance of Macbeth. Yet how many of them would have asked to see it?

We are interested in serving all age groups. For the very young children, there are theatre troupes putting on productions especially for the little ones. They may be jaded by television, but they respond wholeheartedly to real actors and actresses, in make-believe situations. Special showings of films suitable for children fulfill a distinct need in today's entertainment world. Your children, and your community may welcome these with open arms. Can such programs be shown in a high school? Of course! The auditorium is your theatre. The cost for film rental and the projectionist is your major expense. The service to the children and the parents is of great import. Try it and see!

For teenagers and young adults, the same types of programs may be considered. Here are some ideas:

Lectures

There are many famous people who "do the lecture circuit." They may be part of the scene in the big city, but, when they go out into other communities they create quite a stir. Before hiring a lecturer, send a committee to hear him address another audience. An uninspired, dull speaker is not worth the time you are asking people to spend to hear him. On the other hand, a person with verve, fire and a message can capture an audience. We heard Dick Gregory do this, recently. Speaking primarily to high school and college students, his effect was absolutely pyrotechnical!

Choose speakers, too, whose message is timely. How unimportant is last week's newspaper? Topics which are controversial, and vital, will make for stimulated audiences, and a full house. Allow time for questions, and if you can possibly arrange it, have your guest accessible—so that people can meet him—and shake his hand. The thrill of this is tremendous. It accounts for the bruised hands of political candidates after Election Day. Ask your guest to plan to remain for a half-hour or so after he finishes speaking.

Authors often go on the lecture circuit. Should you consider one, be sure his material is in tune with the times, and his subjects of interest—or he may be deadly dull.

Film Classics

A film like "The Good Earth" is as important today as it was thirty years ago, and as entertaining. "A Day at the Races," is still as funny as the day it was released. There are hundreds of films worth seeing again—and again. You may wish to run a Film Festival, using such material—and bringing back the great stars of the past—such as Charlie Chaplin, or Al Jolson. However, a word of caution. There were many films which are not classics, and there is no point to bringing them back. They deteriorate with the years, and they offer little to the viewer except a desire to ridicule them. A classic must, and has, withstood the test of time. Be careful, too, of any political overtones—for there are films which are reactionary in their approach, and unworthy of showing.

We feel it very important, however, to bring out the point that your programs should not compete with the local movie theatre, for example. The school is not in business, nor should it give this impression. If there is any indication that there might be problems in this area, we suggest you find other sources for your entertainment.

Plays

You have many choices in this regard. There are professional touring companies from Broadway productions all over the world, but they tour our nation, as well. While the equipment your auditorium has to offer should be taken into consideration, there are many plays which may be done with relatively unsophisticated resources. Not everyone is able to travel to see a play in New York, but, if it is performed in his own locality, he has the opportunity to see and enjoy it.

Summer stock and experimental theatre groups have expanded their operations, and now many function throughout the United States. You may have one, or develop one, in your area, if your school offers the necessary facilities. Often these groups will do Broadway plays with visiting "stars," which may add to the interest considerably. It is important to select plays which have moral and social as well as entertainment value.

In either event, it is worthwhile to introduce your young people to the magic of the theatre. New Yorkers are tremendously fortunate to have a traveling group of Shakespearean players perform—in the summer in parks throughout the city, and for the remainder of the year in the public schools. We mentioned Macbeth. We shall never forget the absorbed expression on the children's faces. The productions are unbelievably professional—in every aspect. Scenery is brought it, and the costumes and make-up are perfect. The actors are absolutely tremendous.

Music

Concerts of all varieties are possible and valuable. The Philharmonic Orchestras of various cities go on tours, as do many of the truly great artists of our time. Chamber music or operatic excerpts may be selected, but do not expect large audiences. If you need these, because of your budgetary expenses, include such programs as folk-singers, who will attract the young people—in droves.

Light opera and musical comedies are possibilities. However, these are usually large extravaganzas, more difficult and costly to produce than you may be able to afford.

Our young people need exposure to good music; many classical selections appeal to them, provided they are introduced in the correct way. If they are going to hear a professional musician, possibly their music teachers can orient them by playing similar pieces of music, or compositions by the same composer. Musical tastes must be developed, and the child who becomes involved with classical music stands to enrich his entire life a great deal.

Dance programs—modern, interpretive, or ballet—are worthy of introduction to your students and to your community. For some children, they are the "Open Sesame" to an entire world, one which will give them pleasure for many, many years. Touring companies are often available, and sometimes extremely exciting.

In planning any program, arrange for adequate publicity. The most exciting speaker is discouraged by a small audience, and a half-empty hall is unpleasant for any performer to behold. These should be avoided by announcing the events well in advance, using posters, sending home reminders, and putting items into the local newspapers. Press releases for your use are available if the performer has a booking agent.

The provision of entertainment by the school, or by a group

using the school's facilities, is a service to young and old alike. It can answer the age-old querry, "Where shall we go tonight?" The older generation may, or may not, decide to take advantage of the opportunities; for the young, anxious to go and to do, this can make the difference between acceptable and anti-social behavior. One of our tasks should be to help our boys and girls to find pursuits of interest, pursuits they will enjoy, and pursuits which will keep them out of trouble.

In 1962, Charles H. Silver, who was Executive Assistant to the Mayor (of the City of New York), for Education and Industrial Development, expressed his feelings thusly in a letter to Governor Rockefeller:

"On November 14 (1962) I counseled Mayor Wagner to discuss with the City Board of Education the urgency of opening at least 200 more school buildings late afternoons and evenings from Monday through Friday, and all day on Saturday and Sunday including evenings so that we can channel the confined energy of our youth into worthwhile educational and recreational projects. I am enclosing a copy of my message to the Mayor, in which I express my belief that youthful crime and delinquency will become much more serious unless we provide for the youngsters in school buildings and on playgrounds a refuge from the narrow, trafficked, slum streets and the over-crowded rooms of their tenement houses and apartments. Rural and suburban young people at least have empty lots and fields. Cities do not have these open areas and must, therefore, compensate our youngsters in the kind of way I propose.

I stressed in my letter to Mayor Wagner that personnel and operation and maintenance of these additional open buildings will involve additional costs, but that the cost will never be as high as the expense of delinquency and correction institutions. Our youth is a human resource precious not only to our City but to our State and Nation. I know that you will agree that we must provide the funds for the opportunity I am proposing.

Accordingly, I urge you to ask the Legislature for new funds to aid cities like ours in efforts to open more public buildings and playgrounds for directing natural youthful vitality into productive educational and recreational projects. City school districts in our

State find it difficult to support adequately even the basic day school programs and, therefore, experience frustration when they consider the maintenance of after-school and weekend activities. But, Mr. Governor, wholesome and constructive after-school and weekend release for the bottled energies of our youth must somehow be provided to avoid their explosion into avenues of crime, delinquency and other social waste. Your leadership in appropriating new State funds for this purpose is essential."

Is it not of paramount importance that we, as educators, foster such programs, if we are to really meet the needs of our boys and girls?

Evaluating Your Program 14

In evaluating any program, curricular or extracurricular, the particular needs of the individual children composing your student body must be of paramount importance, and the unique needs of the entire community considered carefully and realistically. It is absolutely impossible to think of any school program without thinking of the boys and girls in it—for they must be foremost in our minds at all times. A school is nothing without its children, and the school's entire orientation must be around the children attending it. A fine program for one school may be very poor for another. Please keep this basic factor in mind. If your student activities program is helping your students to learn, to grow and develop, to experience democratic processes, to broaden their horizons and to become social, comfortable human beings, then it is a fine program. If you are teaching only subject matter, only reading, writing and arithmetic, you are falling far short!

The needs of the community, too, should affect the offerings and functioning of your school, and particularly of the student activities program. Obviously the needs of the students and the community in a disadvantaged area will differ in many respects from those in middle and upper socio-economic sections. It is the task of the administration of every school to study these needs, and to attempt to fulfill some of them. This involves enlarging the scope of the student activities program, and bringing in many new concepts and techniques.

The process of evaluation should be a constant one, an on-going process which, like a ring, has neither beginning nor end. It should be pragmatic, and experimental in approach. If an idea proves to be worthwhile, it should be utilized, and, if need be, built upon. If it proves to be unsatisfactory, it should be revised, improved upon or eliminated. However, if you feel something has value, give it a fair trial. Don't eliminate it immediately, for there are many fine programs which start slowly. They require time for word of them to spread, and for enthusiasm to build.

We are dealing with many tangibles, and many intangibles. We will attempt to be as specific as possible, but how can we measure morale and school spirit? Do you consider a decrease in the number of broken windows to be of significance? In many areas it is one of the most important criteria. Children's attitudes are easily discussed, more difficult to measure. Parental attitudes, and faculty attitudes, too, carry great weight. Each can give us clues to the climate within the school, and to the effectiveness of the student activities program which so greatly affects it. The climate of a school is reflected in many ways. Are the boys and girls smiling? Are they, for the most part, cooperative? When a faculty member asks them to pick up a piece of paper, for example, do they do it, or give him an argument? In every school there will be some children who are hostile, but is this true of many of the students in your school, or few? We have found that boys who are much taller and more physically mature than their classmates have problems because of their size. But, if they are members of the basketball team, they manage to adjust to school far better, and the problems are minimized. They rarely act with hostility, because they have been given status, and made to feel important. What about your young men? Are they with you, or agin' you?

Are your children's lives built, in some measure, around the student activities program? How many remain in the building after the dismissal bell rings at three? Does the custodian have to chase them out at five or six, or whenever he locks up? These are some of the questions we suggest you ask yourself, in regard to the student activities program in general. Let us now examine your program, with the specific aspects of the extracurricular offerings in mind.

THE STUDENT GOVERNMENT

Does your school have a Student Government? (It may, of course, be called a General Organization, G.O., or by any other name.)

Are the officers and representatives elected by every child in the school?

Is there a spirited campaign before the elections?

After the elections, do the officers and representatives really function effectively in these roles? Do they really have work to do?

Are the children who make up the remainder of the student body kept aware of the work of the officers and representatives?

What are some of the projects and work the Student Government accomplishes?

From the answers to these questions, you have some means of judging the efficacy of the Student Government as it is functioning, or malfunctioning in your school. These questions, we believe, apply to any school, in any area. All children need this training, in the democratic process.

THE CLASS GOVERNMENT

For democracy on the grass roots level, children need to work in the close confines of the classroom. Let us see if the children in your school do.

Does each class elect officers?

Do the teachers permit and encourage these officers to function? (This applies to every class, not just the "good classes.")

Have the officers been able to develop a measure of control over the class—when the need arises?

Have the classes done any sort of philanthropic work? Is there evidence of this visible in the classrooms?

Do your children feel their class government is functional and worthwhile? (Ask them to answer this question in their Language Arts classes, in the form of a short paragraph. Suggest they include the pros and cons. For truly objective replies, you may decide to ask them not to sign their names.)

Assure your teachers that the replies are not to be considered threats to them. Indeed there are many fine teachers who have difficulty providing the opportunity for democracy in action, until they become aware they have not, and make a conscious effort to do so.

THE CLUB PROGRAM

Did you poll the children to determine their interests?

Were you able to set up clubs which the children wanted?

Were you able to discover talents in teachers and students to utilize in this program?

Are members of the community serving as leaders?

How many children are involved in clubs, attending meetings and really participating—at the mid point of the school year? (Registration at this point should reflect, more accurately than at any other time, the actual number of members. It would have been higher at the very onset of the program, but there are many children who, being children, lose interest—through no fault of the club leader. There are, of course, those who drop out because the club is not going well, or for personal reasons. But, by the middle of the year, attendance usually has stabilized.)

Once, toward the end of the term or year, you may wish to have the children fill out a questionnaire. Here are some questions you may wish to ask:

1. To which clubs do you belong?

2. Do you enjoy going to meetings?

3. Do you have friends in the club?

4. Have you made new friends there?

5. Would you join this particular club again next year—if you were able to?

6. What was the most exciting activity in which the club took part?

7. What, if anything, do you think should be done, to improve the club?

8. Were you disappointed in this club, for any reason? If so, why?

In this case, too, we would suggest anonymity. It is far easier to tell the truth without fear of reprisals. We have found that chil-dren will really be honest under such circumstances.

TEAMS AND CHEERLEADERS

Have you established a series of teams in which those children who enjoy competitive sports can participate?

Have you tried to include children who need this type of ac-tivity—for achievement, and for status? (Those who are sometimes discipline problems.)

Have you established teams other than varsity, enabling chil-dren *other* than those who are most skilled, to take part?

Have the teams and cheerleaders caught the imagination of a great many of the boys and girls? Do many apply for membership? Do many attend games?

Is there school spirit engendered by the team, and its results?

Do the parents and members of the community actively support the teams?

Have the boys and girls been taught to be good losers as well as good winners? Do they represent the school well when they attend games "away" from their home school?

THE TUTORIAL PROGRAM

The after-school tutorial program may be one of the most im-portant means of improving education within your school. How can you tell if it is effective?

How many children, at the middle of the year, are attending the tutorial classes? (We should not be overly influenced by numbers but they are surely one criterion to use.)

Consider each child in the group above. Send a note to the teacher of the subject in which he is being tutored, asking her if she has seen improvement in the child's work. Ask, too, if his attitude has improved, and if he has gained some self-confidence as a result of this program. Has his grade level, in terms of standardized testing, improved?

Interview a random sampling of the children, asking them the same questions as those listed above.

You may wish, also, to ask the children to write a short letter to you, tell you about the tutoring, and what they learned from it.

Have you been able to staff this program with some members of the commmunity?

Have the standardized test results of the school, as a whole, improved?

Discuss with your faculty members the results of the tutoring program, with a view toward improving it. Ask them for specific suggestions.

Have the members of the tutorial program give you a summary of what they believe they have accomplished. Ask them to include new techniques they may have learned of, or developed. Request samples of any materials they have developed, and have them give you some idea of the audio-visual equipment they may have used. If they showed filmstrips, ask for a one sentence comment on them. Try to get a summary of the goals and objectives each one had in mind, and the extent to which these were reached.

PUBLICATIONS

Since publications serve two functions—to communicate with the student body and with their parents, and to provide outlets for the creative children, these objectives should be reflected in your survey.

Does your publication speak for your children, in your school—reflecting their thoughts and emotions?

Do they seek to use this as an outlet for their creative energies? Are there many contributors?

Do the teachers encourage the children to submit materials? All of the teachers? (To get each teacher to work with his classes to submit materials may be a task for the administration for it is a very important one.)

—Official Photograph, Board of Education, City of New York

PRIDE IN THEIR ACHIEVEMENT

Student editors of the school magazine *Bridges* receive the Columbia Scholastic Press Award.

Do your students support your advertising campaign?

Is each issue of the newspaper, or *the* issue of the literary magazine or yearbook greeted with enthusiasm? Do you see children reading it in the school building? Do they discuss its contents? Are "letters to the Editor" submitted in response to some of the articles included?

Is the resultant publication one of which the community may be proud?

Do children volunteer for the staff?

Do you give the faculty advisors sufficient time to prepare the work with the youngsters?

PRODUCTIONS

Who chooses the material to be produced?

Do children volunteer for these productions?

Does the public support them—by their attendance?

Are the productions satisfying—not necessarily professionally perfect, but not embarrassingly poor?

Do those productions reflect the work of many of the children?

Is there a climate of excitement in the air before the production?

Are there some children involved who have shown they have problems—who are difficult to manage in the classroom situation?

Do the members of the community support the production?

Do the productions have moral and social significance as well as entertainment value?

THE EVENT-OF-THE-YEAR

Does it catch the interest of the children?

Are the majority of them included?

Does the faculty approve of the event, and support it?

Do the parents support it? Do they attend? Do they contribute their talents?

What new ideas and concepts are developed for the event?

Is it looked forward to, from year to year? By students and by faculty? By parents?

What is the reaction of the members of the community to it?

What, in the opinion of the teachers, is the most valuable aspect of the event? Why (The reasons are important.)

THE EVENING SCHOOL PROGRAM

How many students are participating at the mid-point of the year?

How many parents and community members are involved, at that time of the year?

Does the program show growth from year to year?

Which courses are offered as a direct result of the polling of students and members of the community?

How many people reregister, from year to year?

Analyze the courses being offered. Are they courses which are furthering the education of the students? Do they show cultural growth?

Ask the students in the program to answer the following questions:

1. Why did you take this course?
2. Are you learning what you wished to learn from it?
3. Would you recommend it to your best friend? Why?
4. Are you, in any way, disappointed in it?
5. What aspects of it made you particularly happy?
6. Do you feel it could be improved? If so, how?
7. Is there any information which you needed, and which you were not able to get? What?

THE SCHOOL AS A SOCIAL CENTER

1. Have you considered extending the offerings of the school to meet the needs of your community?

2. Have you supplied places for the children to congregate after dismissal time?

3. Are you aware of the number of children who use this place?

4. Have you attempted to bring into the school, and make welcome, the parents and members of the community? In what ways have you done this?

5. Have you given thought to the senior citizens in the area, with the idea in mind that they might use the school as a meeting place?

6. Have you tried to bridge the generation gap by bringing children and adults together?

After you have worked out and obtained the answers to the questions listed, you are in a position to review your program. It is obvious that, in spite of this attempted objectivity, you will have to be subjective in your approach, as well. Remember, please, that no program is ever perfect. There is rarely even one which cannot, in some way, be improved. However, the interest and enthusiasm of the children is far more important than the perfection of the performance. Every activity is subject to the effect of human nature, and when we are dealing with children, the most unpredictable results should not surprise us. They respond to many stimuli of which we may not even be aware.

You must, of course, determine whether your funding is being used to the best advantage. For this, you must consider the benefits accruing—and consider this, please, in terms of the numbers of children involved, and also the benefits each receives. We know of one club in which there are less than ten members. The leader is a perfect father-image (although, unfortunately he has no children)—*but every single child, except one, in the club has no father.* He has taken the place of the male absent from their lives. Could you say that the funding for this club would have to be cut because of the limited number of students? This would be nothing short of tragic—for those children.

Give every activity a fair chance to succeed. In order to do this, we suggest you do not eliminate any aspect entirely, after one year of operation. Some of the most successful activities take longer than that to really catch on. If, after several years you find the activity has not grown and developed, you may wish to combine it with something else. This is particularly true of the club program, for example.

You may wish to meet with other administrators to discuss the student activities program in their schools. This is always an excellent source of ideas—for, as programs develop, new concepts come to the fore. As simple a discussion as "What musical comedies have you put on which proved to be successful?" can really help. We have found replies in the negative to be as valuable as those which are positive. If a play is indifferently received in another school, consider carefully how it will be received in yours. Many productions are overly long—and become boring as a result.

From your colleagues you may be able to elicit helpful information in regard to which clubs were the most successful, which evening courses the most desirable, and ideas for an event-of-the-year. Try comparing notes, and new thoughts will surely be developed.

This cooperative method is used constantly in private industry to generate ideas.

Do the children and parents seem happy? Are they enthusiastic? Have you seen an improvement in the attitudes of the children as they go about their daily work? Has the effect upon the discipline been wholesome and salutary? Do you find many of the children remaining after the dismissal bell? Has a spirit of rapport been developed? What are the parents' comments about the students activities program when they visit the school? What are their reactions when the extracurricular program is discussed at Parent Association meetings?

What reputation does the school enjoy in the community? Are people anxious and willing to enter its portals? What suggestions are offered for the improvement of this program?

Has the school contributed in any way to the growth and development of the community? Have you brought into the school life new ideas and concepts, and have you put them into operation? Have you strengthened the rapport between the teachers, the administration and the community? Can you honestly say the program has benefited most of the children in the school?

CONCLUSION

Education must concern itself, in the remainder of the twentieth century, with those changes which will enable us to keep up with the times. One of our most important goals must be the development of the whole person, and in this development the student activities program must play a most important role. Teaching subject matter and skills is only one part of our task, a fraction of the total development. The child has psychological as well as physical needs, which must be fulfilled if he is to grow into a well-adjusted, successful human being . . . a whole person. The extracurricular activities such as teams or clubs are instrumental in achieving this because they offer many, many opportunities for experiencing feelings of belonging. The child who needs assistance if he is to experience success academically will benefit greatly from the tutorial program, and possibly from the class and student governments, for very often it is the non-academically oriented child who is elected to office. Creative boys and girls may take advantage of the possibilities to achieve which working on the school newspaper and literary magazine offers to them. Young people seem to crave the friendship of their peers, and all of the extracurricular activities provide this. The entire program is geared toward developing the children's proclivities and talents. Here we lean, not toward subject matter, but toward the children's gifts.

The student activities program thus affords us with many opportunities which the regular curriculum cannot possibly include. It gives us chances to become close to our children, and to get to know one another as individuals, on a people-to-people basis. It gives many children, who would never have it otherwise, the chance to shine, and offers companionship to the lonely child, and a recognition of his gifts which might otherwise go unnoticed, and even unknown to the child himself. The young people are given a "say" in the voice of the government of their school, something for which they are now clamoring. For the teachers, the student activities program furnishes the means by which they can get closer to the children, and thereby possibly gain a better understanding of them.

By extending the student activities program to include the members of the community, in the evening schools, and in the social centers, we achieve community involvement in a most wholesome way, bringing together children and adults, and thus bridging the generation gap. Discussions are encouraged, differences aired, and harmonious relationships fostered.

The physical health of the children is also improved, for exercise and activity are the keynotes, today, of health and well-being. The social graces are learned through practice, and not by preaching, making the children more comfortable in various types of situations. This learning will be of great value to them long after they have left the school.

We must then encourage our students, be they children or adults, to engage in the physical, intellectual and spiritual endeavors that abound in the student activities program, for it is through this extracurricular program that we, as educators, can work to reach many of the most worthwhile goals of education.

For example, through our school and class governments, we enable our children to live democracy, instead of studying about it. Through our clubs and various productions, we are offering creative outlets, and providing the impetus for original work. Through our newspapers, and literary magazines, we supply a forum for the expression of ideas, the ideas the children are often so anxious to communicate. In the tutorial program, we are able to unite the efforts of the youngsters, the parents and the teachers in eliminating ignorance; by establishing situations in which the children and adults work harmoniously together, we can strive to defeat bigotry and its incredible cruelties and injustices; by providing many opportunities for companionship, we combat loneliness and its accompanying evils. Above all, we must never forgot that the student activities program, like every other program associated with education, must teach justice, unity, and most important, compassion for one's fellow man.

Index